W9-AZT-091

ICE

BOREALIS
BOOKS

ICE

Great Moments in the History
of Hard, Cold Water

KARAL ANN MARLING

Borealis Books is an imprint of the Minnesota Historical Society Press.
www.borealisbooks.org

The Minnesota Historical Society Press is a member of the Association of American University
Presses.

Manufactured in the United States of America

10   9   8   7   6   5   4   3   2   1

♾ The paper used in this publication meets the minimum requirements of the American
National Standard for Information Sciences—Permanence for Printed Library Materials, ANSI
Z39.48–1984.

International Standard Book Number
ISBN 13: 978-0-87351-628-0 (cloth)
ISBN 10: 0-87351-628-1 (cloth)

Library of Congress Cataloging-in-Publication Data
Marling, Karal Ann.
    Ice : great moments in the history of hard, cold water / Karal Ann Marling.
        p. cm.
    Includes bibliographical references and index.
    ISBN-13: 978-0-87351-628-0 (cloth : alk. paper)
    ISBN-10: 0-87351-628-1 (cloth : alk. paper)
    1. Ice—History. 2. Ice—Social aspects. 3. Ice—Popular works. I. Title.
    GB2405.M27 2008
    551.31—dc22
2008010632

Book design and typesetting by Percolator, Minneapolis
Printed by Sheridan Books, Inc., Ann Arbor

"I looked out at the icebergs.
They were so beautiful they . . . made you afraid."

—

Barry Lopez, *Arctic Dreams*

CONTENTS

ICE

BREAKING THE ICE

"Put your mittens on! You'll freeze to death!"

—

Folk warning from the world's grandmothers

Mothers and grandmothers say that a lot when winter catches the states along the Canadian border in its icy grip and, almost overnight, everything outdoors sets up harder than a fresh Popsicle. Old ladies get out their L. L. Bean catalogs: it's time to order a pair of those steel-toothed "grippers," worn over last year's zip-up-the-middle snow boots to insure traction on slippery sidewalks. It's cold and getting colder. Icicles hang from sagging gutters like the daggers of the angry gods of Thule. Semi-lethal snowballs—the ones with lumps of ice buried inside—are stockpiled out behind the garage. As Moms fuss over mittens, kids pour buckets of water on the driveway to make an instant ice slide. Fathers curse mightily when the new all-weather tires fail to propel the family car up that same ice slide. It's winter in the Northland. Now put those mittens on or you'll freeze to death out there!

There is no evidence that the mothers of the great Arctic and Antarctic explorers tendered similar advice. Scott, Peary, Shackleton, and the other rimed heroes of the Heroic Age of polar adventuring seem to have figured out that mitts, gloves, mittens, and the like were a good idea as the temperatures plummeted to 80 degrees below. Oddly, however, the British among them insisted that woolen uniforms were far better than Inuit furs simply because the uniforms were British. As a result, many a brave Victorian hero was "nipped" to death by ice-laden winds while man-hauling a heavy sled or buried alive in bottomless crevasses in the glacial surface before the scions of the Royal Geographic Society finally decided it was best to wear furs and drive dog teams. By then, however, the show was pretty much over.

I'm an Ice Baby myself, not to be confused with a Snow Baby. "Snow Baby" was the title the press bestowed on the infant daughter of Robert Peary, putative discoverer of the North Pole. Little Marie was born in 1893 only 13° from the pole, where Peary's missus had spent the later months of her pregnancy cavorting on the ice floes near the top of the world. Newspaper reports noted that Marie was the first *white* child born so far to the north and, therefore, a phenomenon. The *other* Snowbabies, currently manufactured in bulk by a Minnesota giftware firm, are china figurines of adorable tykes wearing snowsuits that seem to have been made of snow lumps and ice crystals. They are, in my opinion, exceedingly creepy.

Thank heavens I'm an Ice Baby, born in the deep-freeze belt of upstate New York and resident for more than thirty years in Minnesota. Need I say more? I grew up at a time when an iceman with a horse made twice-a-week home deliveries, in a place where children stood around neighborhood ponds with rosary beads the day after Halloween (All Saints' Day) praying for the skating rink to ice over. Now I live in a place where the lakes' annual "ice-out" is an event of hold-the-presses magnitude. And ice amounts to the state logo of Minnesota. Henry Wadsworth Longfellow never made it as far west

Ice formation, 1875

as Minnehaha Creek, but as he imagined Hiawatha and his world in 1855, the poet got it absolutely right. "When I blow my breath about me," says the north wind, "When I breathe upon the landscape, / Motionless are all the rivers, / Hard as stone becomes the water!"

I have a theory about water hard as stone. A one-time hockey player too proud to buy grippers, I have never really managed to get my ice legs under me without my skates. If there is ice to be slipped on, I'm there, flat on my back, looking up at the cold blue sky. Now, if a person takes a header on concrete—while wearing in-line skates, for example—the damage is almost always substantial: sprains, casts, bloody bandages. But the same tumble on water hard as stone leaves you breathless and giddy but rarely in the emergency room. That's because sidewalks do their damage by friction, whereas a fall on ice is deflected at the moment of impact by blessed slipperiness. The victim slides off to the side. Gravity is defeated. No harm done. Ice is good. I'm not in the camp of those who call city hall to complain when the guy next door fails to de-ice his sidewalk with chemical goo while the flakes are still flying.

My favorite movie scene of all time comes in *A Christmas Story* (1983), when "Flick," the hero's pal, licks the grade school flagpole on a dare and freezes his tongue to the metal. That's my idea of cinema verité! I can't present myself to you, Dear Reader, as a scientific expert on ice. I'm a theorist, a partisan, a historian, and an aficionado of ice. I will not be moving to Arizona for the winter (although I do often summer in Alaska). If a sooty, hot-blooded Vulcan offers me an ice-cream cone during the St. Paul Winter Carnival parade while a stiff breeze zooming straight from Siberia threatens to weld the trumpets to the lips of passing band members, I'll grab that cone. Mmmm. Mmmm. Ice cream! Even if I have to peel off my mittens to get a good grip on it.

Ice storm in Minneapolis, 1952

1

ICE SWEET ICE

"I Scream, You Scream"

—

Ancient advertising slogan

Water freezes at 32 degrees Fahrenheit (a scale of measurement named for the inventor of the mercury thermometer). Simply put, at 32°F water turns into a solid. And when frozen, that water expands in volume. It can become sparkly and slick. It is very cold to the touch. Snowflakes are hexagonal ice crystals on their way to becoming either glaciers or slush. But ordinary, everyday ice comes to the party in cubes, chunks, or chips. Jokesters serve highballs over ice frozen into the shape of busty Playboy bunnies. People with a compulsion to chew ice of whatever shape are called *pagophagiacs;* they often suffer from bad teeth. People with a compulsion to eat ice cream—and Popsicles and the like—are simply sensible, if sometimes chubby. In the words of one thoughtful ice-creamophile, "All ice cream is good."

> At the 2007 Kentucky Derby, one bar offered a special $1,000 mint julep. The cup was gold-plated, the straw was silver, the bourbon was aged and smooth. The real attraction? It was served over ice imported from above the **ARCTIC CIRCLE**.

Historians who have studied the origins of frozen comestibles have an impressive stockpile of myths, half-truths, and maybes at their disposal. Marco Polo, for example, is said to have brought the secret of ice cream back with him from China in the thirteenth century, along with a goodly supply of spaghetti. Yet the extant Tang Dynasty recipe for a kind of semi–ice cream calls for fermenting a mixture of milk and ground rice and then adding flour (for thickening) and camphor (for flavor). Camphor is the stuff that keeps moths out of winter clothes and makes liniments smell as if they must be working. Camphor ice cream sounds disgusting, even if the emperor of China did keep the ninety-four icemen in his retinue busy cooling the odd confection.

Ancient European history is rife with examples of monarchs and merchants importing mountain snow during the off-season to cool their libations and make frozen delicacies. Wealthy Athenians of the fifth century BC bought snow in their city markets, if only to flaunt their riches. Alexander the Great stored snow in earthen pits so his armies could enjoy refreshing summer drinks. Nero sent slaves to Mount Etna, instructing them to run all the way back to Rome before the precious snow could melt away. The sketchy descriptions of classical-era desserts made from snow suggest something like today's Italian ices or classier versions of the slurpee or the sno-cone doctored with honey, fruit, and wine.

An ice cream that approximated the real thing came later, perhaps via the Chinese and Marco Polo or through the good offices of Arab traders who stopped their caravans in Italy on their way home from China (or some other remote and exotic spot, such as Sicily or Egypt). In any case, around 1559 genuine ice cream appeared in Naples, where the "secret" of mixing ice with salt to freeze milk or cream was discovered. Salt, which raises the boiling point of water, can also lower the freezing point of liquids below 32°F, the so-called endothermic effect. When the ice-salt mixture is colder than cold, the resulting chill can be transferred to other substances by conduction. Using the still pot method, a metal container filled with milk, sugar, and a tasty extract is placed in a larger vessel holding a mixture of salt and ice.

After watching, shaking the ice, and stirring the pot to incorporate bits that have begun to adhere to its sides, the result is ice cream.

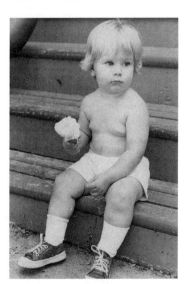

Boy with cone, 1974

Ice cream made by the pot method was a labor-intensive treat. All that tending and scraping required armies of faithful retainers, to say nothing of the servants dispatched to higher altitudes in the summer months in search of more ice. So, until the eighteenth century, ice cream consumption was mainly a king's prerogative. Charles I bribed a French chef for exclusive rights to the process; the French had learned the pot method from the Italians through the good offices of Henry II, who married a Medici. In any case, ice cream remained a semi-secret luxury. During a banquet at Windsor Castle in 1672, Charles II (who also commandeered the first pineapple grown in England) got a plate of ice cream to go with his strawberries. Everybody else sat and watched him eat it.

From London, ice cream migrated to the New World. A copy of the *New-York Gazetteer* for November 23, 1773, contains a variety of ads for whale blubber, soap, candles, and rheumatism pills. There is also a notice of a new business in the offing: a Monsieur Lenzi, Confectioner, who had catered "in most of the principal cities of Europe," promised to have ice cream for sale to customers planning "Balls, Masquerades &c." George Washington's ledgers show that he purchased two hundred dollar's worth of ice cream—a lot of it!—in New York City during his presidency, presumably to entertain guests at his official receptions or, more elegantly put, "levees." An inventory of the contents of Mount Vernon after Washington's death in 1799 included no fewer than ten ice-cream pots, two made of pewter and the rest of tin, along with a silver ice-cream spoon. There were also thirty-six small, footed "ice cups" of French chinaware for serving a dessert that tended to arrive at the table in a somewhat soupy condition during a typical Virginia summer.

One of the most persistent tall tales about ice cream holds that Martha Washington, for reasons lost to history, left a bowl of cream and sugar on her back porch on a cold evening and came back in the morning to find a bowl of ice cream. Not true. Ice cream is no accident of nature. The Library of Congress has Thomas Jefferson's exacting recipe for making vanilla ice cream in a pot, scrawled in his distinctive hand in the 1780s. Written on the back of the sheet is Jefferson's own recipe for Savoy cookies to finish off the dessert. America's first certified gourmand and a lover of all things French, Jefferson came home from his travels abroad with the formulas for many foods that have become typically American, including "French" fries, macaroni and cheese, and a rich ice cream made with a custard based on the addition of six egg yolks (and beaten in a Gallic pot called a *sorbetière*). Most of the ingredients for the Jeffersonian custard mixture were readily obtained from his own lands at Monticello. The struggle was to procure whole vanilla beans or, as he phrased it in urgent letters to agents in Paris and elsewhere, "batons" of what would become his nation's favorite ice cream flavor.

Dolley Madison, the Quaker wife of President James Madison, confirmed the developing connection between patriotism and ice cream. Reputed to be a slave to fashion in all matters, she electrified the city of Washington by serving ice cream with strawberries to the masses at her husband's second inaugural ball in 1812. A guest at a Madison dinner party later in the year—before the British burned down the White House—reported the general astonishment when the table was seen to contain "in the centre high on a silver platter, a large, shining dome of pink ice cream." Rumor has it that Dolley learned the secrets of ice cream from "Aunt Sallie Shadd," a freed slave living in Wilmington, Delaware. Given its prevalence as the *ne plus ultra* of presidential entertaining, however, that story is suspect.

> The austere Abraham Lincoln was equally fond of **SHAKE-SPEARE** and **ICE CREAM**.

More significant for the spread of ice cream from the White House to everybody's house was the invention of the hand-cranked freezer, still in use today. Consisting of a bucket to hold the ice, a metal container for the cream, a lid penetrated by a crank for stirring the custard, and a dasher turned by the crank that scraped the sides of the "pot" while the freezing took place, the home freezer made the whole process a lot easier. The apparatus was the brainchild of Nancy M. Johnson of Philadelphia. Johnson has been identified over the years as a "New England housewife" and a resident of New Jersey, all on the slenderest of evidence. It is now certain, however, that she patented her "artificial freezer" in 1843 (patent number 3254) from a Philadelphia address.

It was once believed, too, that she was somehow cheated out of her invention. Another myth. But within the thirty-year period after the Johnson patent was registered, more than seventy designs for "improved" versions of her product were marketed. And the tradition of ice cream—usually vanilla—for church socials, Fourth of July picnics, and bridal receptions originated with Nancy Johnson's easy-to-use machine. Jacob Fussell, a Baltimore dairyman who found himself unable to produce more than two quarts of ice cream a day using the old pot method, seems to have been the first to manufacture ice cream on an industrial scale by attaching a flywheel to the freezer crank around 1851. Now, ice cream could be taken to the streets. Enter the "hokeypokey" man.

Hokeypokey men—usually Italian immigrants—sold something cold and white and ice-cream-like from push-carts on the streets of urban America in the post–Civil War era. They had been preceded by rough, curbside stands where the poorest of the city's poor sold all manner of cheap goods by shouting catchy phrases at passersby. In 1828, a Washington newspaper recorded the chant of one such vendor. "I Scream Ice Cream," he screamed, as he served up his penny-licks: one cent bought a tiny portion of a dubious product that passed for a chilly taste of heaven on the capital's steaming streets. In fact, ice cream sold in this way was rarely made from cream. Shaken and scraped on the spot, under the most unsanitary conditions imaginable, it was often tainted with contagions.

So, although *hokeypokey* became a universal synonym for ice cream of the lowest quality (stiffened with gelatin, arrowroot, or flour), Italian street hawkers seem to have raised the general level of purity. Nobody is sure where the singsong name of the hokeypokey men came from. Perhaps it is a crude, Americanized version of the phrase *"O, che poco,"* meaning "how cheap" or "just a little lick." For a penny, that is precisely what the customer got—a lick, eaten straight from the serving spoon, dumped on a square of brown paper, or scooped into a tiny glass with steep sides and a flat bottom and wiped out with a towel between customers if you were lucky. "Here's the stuff to make you jump," they cried. "Hokeypokey, penny a lump!"

Meanwhile, on the higher rungs of the social ladder, ice cream was putting on airs. Dolley Madison's dome of pink ice cream was evolving into elegant, expensive "shapes" or molds, sure to delight the guests on important occasions. In keeping with the Victorian fondness for elaborate and time-consuming culinary decor—and surprises—ice cream was refrozen in pewter or copper molds to resemble elephants, baskets of flowers, club insignias, or tiny chicks (in nests of spun sugar). Every season had its own George Washington hatchets, St. Patrick's Day potatoes, Easter eggs and bunnies, and Independence Day red-white-and-blue flags. Sometimes, whole cakes were filled and frosted with ice cream; these were properly known as "society puddings."

The master of the art was Charles Ranhofer, a chef at the famous Delmonico's restaurant in New York City. He came up with a whole range of new ice cream flavors to tempt the jaded palates of the Four Hundred, including asparagus and pumpernickel rye bread. If these were not unusual enough, Ranhofer often brought his oddest creations to the table wearing trompe l'oeil disguises. Asparagus ice cream, for instance, was presented as a plate of asparagus spears daintily tied together with a pink (strawberry?) ribbon. He also specialized in ice cream tomatoes, mushrooms, and ears of corn. Early in the twentieth century, three major U.S. firms were making fancy molds for caterers and for adventurous home cooks. Holiday shapes, like Santas and bells, were popular but so were fruits (life size or in miniature) and flowers, recommended for bridge club gatherings and spring nuptials. Today, the outlines of shamrocks and Christmas angels once embedded in bricks of store-bought ice cream have migrated to tubes of slice-and-bake cookie dough. Ice cream molding is a lost art.

Ranhofer's most lasting contribution to his trade was not asparagus ice cream but a lovely creation known as Baked Alaska, first popularized at Delmonico's. A combination of cake and ice cream covered in a crust of meringue and served up hot from the oven seems magical but is, at the most, a matter of good timing. The trick is knowing that egg whites are heat resistant, an idea that probably

originated with the scientist Benjamin Thompson of Wo-
burn, Massachusetts, in the late 1700s. (Persian scholars of
ancient times had already invented a substance made of egg
whites, sand, ashes, and the like to coat underground spaces
for storing ice in the desert.) Ranhofer called the first version of Baked Alaska "Alaska-Florida" in his own 1893 cook-
book. It consisted of a frozen core of cake topped off with
banana (Florida) and vanilla (Alaska) ice creams. Culinary
historians claim that Baked Alaska was so called in honor of
William H. Seward's purchase of the territory from Russia
in 1867. It seems more likely, however, that the great Klondike gold rush of 1896 had something to do with the name
under which the dish most often appeared in cookbooks
published after 1900 or so. In the 1950s, when Alaskas were
revived in the new, all-electric kitchens of suburbia, house-
wives were urged to improve upon the original by shaping
their creations into little igloos.

Avoiding street vendors and high-society asparagus
spears, respectable middle-class America gravitated to the
ice cream saloons and soda fountains that were established
institutions before Ranhofer ever dreamt of Baked Alaska.
Flavored or "plain," cold, tingly, bubbly water was a miracle
of nineteenth-century technology and advertising. Unlike the
naturally carbonated waters of spas, to which fashionable invalids and scoundrels repaired, commercial seltzers were in-
expensive, readily available close to home, and recommended
for ailments ranging from obesity and dyspepsia to bad nerves.
Fizzy curative waters were created by passing a weak acid
over a source of calcium; the wizard of the soda water business was a New Yorker, John Matthews, who scored a coup by
buying up the marble scraps left over from the construction

of St. Patrick's Cathedral and turning them into twenty-five million gallons of the elixir, which also claimed to be a temperance drink, a super-fire substitute for alcohol.

Soon the soda dispenser or fountain sprang up everywhere, lending the term to establishments in which such artifacts of modern civilization loomed like massive altars to good health. At the 1876 Philadelphia Centennial Exposition, temperance societies banded together to keep alcoholic beverages off the grounds. Instead, ornate multistory soda fountains urged sinners to toss back the healing, ice-cooled waters of repentance. One black marble fountain, called the "Minnehaha" in honor of Longfellow's shining waters, sported columns of silver, urns of bronze, basins, and statuary. The firm of James W. Tufts, who began the practice of embellishing fountains with exotic decorations—and names such as Frost King, Icefloe, and Avalanche—installed a thirty-ton model so tall that it proved impossible to sell until it became, first, a Coney Island attraction and, later, a tourist draw towering over the main floor of a St. Louis department store.

Fairgoers, even those who considered cold beverages hazardous to their health, found the "arctic waters" at the centennial impossible to resist. Coke, Pepsi, and all the rest of our pop machine favorites flow from those awe-inspiring bubble machines. It was probably inevitable, then, that soda fountains, which had begun to add flavoring syrups to their five-cent drinks in the mid-1860s, would come up with the notion of tossing in ice cream, too, during the craze for novelty beverages that swept the country after the Civil War. As manias came and went, they cast up faddish soda concoctions named after passing fancies, like the bicycle craze of the 1880s ("Sprocket Foam"). A 1934 issue of the *Ice Cream Trade Journal* summed it up best: "The ice cream soda is a characteristically American product along with baseball, skyscrapers, hot biscuits, . . . Vermont maple syrup, Negro spirituals, rough-riding cowboys, and hooked rugs."

There are countless pretenders to the title of the first documented ice cream soda magnate. Some insist that the all-American soda was created by accident when a concessionaire at a Philadelphia festival in 1874 ran out of liquid cream for his drinks and was forced to substitute ice cream. Others credit the genesis to the owner of a Detroit drugstore fountain who had the same problem in 1878 (or was it 1858?). Or to a New York City confectioner who catered to newsboys and let the kids experiment with his stock to their hearts' content one slow afternoon in 1872.

The ice cream sundae made its debut during the following decade. Like the soda, it has many putative fathers scattered from Buffalo and Ithaca, New York, to Evanston, Illinois, and Two Rivers, Wisconsin. At least one story insists that the name is a corruption of *Sunday* and that the dish was concocted to overcome pious folks' objections to the consumption of fizzy or "frilly" (hence overly exciting) sodas on the Sabbath. Others believe that an enterprising druggist invented the sundae to perk up slow Sunday sales. The 1915 edition of *The Dispenser's Formulary* contains scores of recipes for gooey combinations of preserved fruit, flavoring syrups, nuts, marshmallows—and ice cream.

One of the most memorable of these was the "Roosevelt Special," named in honor of the vessel in which Robert Peary sailed north for his 1909 assault on the pole. This dazzling treat began with an iceberg of vanilla ice cream topped off with a strawberry ship and, presumably, a flag. Other topical sundaes included a spectacular creation commemorating the new Brooklyn Bridge. Using two cone-shaped scoops of ice cream to construct the bridge towers, the deck—a slice of orange—was carefully suspended between them. The banks of the river were chocolate studded with chopped pecans, the water a stream of mint syrup, and the result a kind of gastronomic nightmare.

Novelty sundaes that looked like skyscrapers or Commodore Perry's fleet passed out of favor over time. What remained was the plain, old, iconic ice-cream cone, which, if it was not seen first at the St. Louis World's Fair of 1904, came into its own one sweltering summer day along the

Eating ice-cream cones in front of "New York to the North Pole," St. Louis World's Fair, 1904

"Pike," the exposition's raucous amusement zone. Charles Menches, an ice cream vendor, ran out of penny-lick dishes with a long line of customers waiting at his stand. He ran to the booth next door, so the story goes, and borrowed some crispy cornucopias of pastry from a Syrian pal, Ernest Hamwi. The ice cream went into the cones. The crowd loved 'em, and another perfect "walking food" took its place on the menu of fair cuisine. The great fairs and festivals of the fin de siècle period—the centennial, the Columbian Exposition, world's fairs in St. Louis and Buffalo, huge state fairs everywhere—gave rise to convenient "hand" edibles, including the hot dog, the hamburger, and the ice-cream cone. Practicality and a growing concern for public health also helped to do away with reusable dishes.

> Fairs are great venues for selling all manner of new, revolutionary, laborsaving gadgets. At the Pan-American Exposition in Buffalo in 1901, the Enterprising Manufacturing Company distributed thousands of free recipe booklets that, not coincidentally, touted its own line of hand-operated kitchen aids. One of them, the **ENTERPRISE ICE SHREDDER**, was a fifty-cent item highly recommended for the fashionable hostess who wished to serve iced tea or oysters on the half shell to her guests.

During the 1960s, an old lady who had attended the St. Louis Fair as a girl of eleven remembered eating an ice-cream cone there, made from a hot waffle rolled into a conical shape. The ice cream "dripped from the hole in the bottom of the cone," but it was delicious, "and we ate it all." Hers may have not been the prototypical ice-cream cone, though. In far-off New York, an Italian newcomer—Italo

Marchioni—patented a similar cone in December 1903. His had a flat bottom and was modeled after the traditional hokeypokey glass. But because St. Louis was a foundry town, local businessmen there were quicker to capitalize on producing baking equipment for cones, either rolled up or made from a batter poured into hot molds. In 1906, one of these new ice-cream cone tycoons served up his product at something called the Modern Woodmen of America Frisco Log Rolling in the town of Sullivan, Missouri. Missouri partisans argue that the Woodmen's convention established the primacy of cones as the modern vehicle for serving ice cream. Perhaps it is best to say that, circa 1900, the ice-cream cone was an idea whose time had finally come.

In time, temperance advocates carried the day. Revivalism and Prohibition cast up a wave of mass-produced and fervently advertised ice cream novelties designed to appease the nation's sweet tooth in a more wholesome and godly manner. Ice Poles, Polar Eggs, Klondike Bars, and Eskimo Pies are among the more enduring brand names of the 1920s. They are reminders of the notoriety of the world's coldest places at the time: the Antarctic, where Robert Falcon Scott froze to death in 1912; the Peary/Cook squabble over the North Pole; the Alaskan gold rush; the release of the Inuit documentary *Nanook of the North* (1922).

> **LONG ISLAND ICED TEA** is a lethal combination of vodka, tequila, rum, gin, and Coke, often containing no tea at all.

The brand names alone affirm the average American's interest in icy, strange, and somehow captivating sensations. The friendly Eskimo on the wrapper of the Eskimo Pie was not its original trademark, however. The brainchild of Christian Nelson, an Iowa teacher-turned-confectioner who watched children dithering over the choice between chocolate bars and ice cream, the first coated slabs of vanilla cream were called "Temptation I-Scream Bars." The homegrown ad slogan was a distant echo of the hokeypokey man's cry: "I scream, you scream, we all scream for the I-Scream Bar!"

On his way to Omaha in 1920 to talk about a patent, Nelson met the future chocolate millionaire Russell Stover, who had better ideas about how to make the candy shell adhere to the ice cream. Stover hated the "I scream" slogan and sent his sister off to the public library on a search for evocative words that said "ice cold" to the man on the street. Cold + dessert = Eskimo Pie! In 1927, the bars were so popular that they were being sold by the millions in nickel slot machines, forerunners of the modern vending machine.

Eskimo pie wrapper

All that remained was for a California businessman of great inventiveness to build (and patent!) a roadside stand in the San Gabriel Valley in the shape of an owl. The bird's head swiveled from side to side. His huge eyes—the headlights from a Cadillac—blinked on and off. "Hoot Hoot I Scream" was emblazoned in massive letters just over the single doorway flanked by Mr. Owl's giant feathered legs.

California was a leader in the field of programmatic architecture—buildings so peculiar, eye-catching, or suggestive of the delights inside as to coax the motorist off the road. When auto tourism increased in the 1920s and '30s, so did the number of roadside oddities like giant igloos flanked by plaster polar bears, two-story ice cream freezers, oversized cardboard take-home cartons, and upside-down cones. The majority of these establishments served ice cream, of course. But others simply used the iconography of ice and ice cream to hint at a cool respite from the heat of an un-air-conditioned touring car. The Eskimo igloo, embedded in an artificial iceberg complete with growling bears, was patented in 1928 by Los Angeles architect John Henry Whitington.

Hoot Hoot Ice Cream, Rosemead, California

Real Eskimos, whose cold-weather habitat calls for an even higher proportion of dietary fat than today's premium ice creams supply, make a substitute—something called *Akutaq.* The recipe calls for adding a quart or two of berries to a mixture of Crisco and sugar. Fluff with a spoon, chill, and enjoy! Akutaq is widely known as Eskimo ice cream. But frigid places seem to spawn an appetite for cold stuff, however un-ice-cream-like it may actually be. A formula designed for folks living in snowy climates recommends blending whipping cream, a dash of vanilla, and some sugar

Polar Bear Custard, Wichita, Kansas, 1938

with "clean, fresh," *white* snow bearing no signs of recent animal activity. Vilhjalmur Stefansson, a leading Arctic explorer of the early twentieth century and a widely published author of books on the life of the Inuit peoples of the north, famously claimed that chewing frozen raw bear meat was just like eating hard ice cream.

> Pagophabia, or the **COMPULSIVE CONSUMPTION OF ICE**, is classified as an eating disorder harmful to both teeth and digestion. Arctic explorers are instructed not to eat ice when thirsty because the amount of heat needed to melt it can produce hypothermia. Experienced trekkers put snow and ice in vessels tucked inside their garments and drink the resulting ice meltwater.

And so it goes. Good Humor men in white uniforms blaring their siren calls for ice cream from their tidy white

trucks. Howard Johnson and his famous twenty-eight flavors (the challenge was to make the clerk recite them out
loud, on the ruse that you were too young to read). Frozen
custard. Dove bars on sticks. Hägen-Dazs. Ben & Jerry and
their pints of Cherry Garcia. Comic Bill Cosby's monologue
about the kid who is talked into having his tonsils out on
the promise that he can eat all the ice cream he wants—
and then he's too sick to manage a single spoonful. Ice
cream is everywhere! People who write about the subject
are, I have learned, a prickly and contentious lot, given to
discrediting each other's statistics and quasi facts. But the
industry itself claims that Americans currently eat more
ice cream per capita in a given year than any other nation
on Earth: twenty-three quarts. I have eaten that much myself, and more, without a moment's regret. A German officer, widely quoted in American newspapers during World
War I, huffed, "We do not fear that nation of ice cream eat-
ers!" Predictably, consumption soared. It was tantamount to
one's patriotic duty to eat more ice cream. It still is, I think.
"I scream, you scream, we all scream for ice cream!"

A patriotic duty: poster, 1914–18

2

OVER THE ICE

"For destruction ice / Is also great"

—

Robert Frost, *Fire and Ice* (1923)

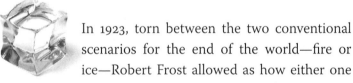 In 1923, torn between the two conventional scenarios for the end of the world—fire or ice—Robert Frost allowed as how either one would do the trick. Fire? Fine. Ice "would suffice," too. Fire reminds the poet of his own hot desire and ice the chill of hatred. For polar explorers of the Heroic Age, for the Amundsens and Scotts and Shackletons, the fires of compulsion were stoked by the very real dangers of ice and snow. Death lurked at the extremes of heat and cold. There is a persistent legend that the *Times* of London ran an advertisement for would-be Antarctic adventurers in 1907: "Bitter cold, long hours of complete darkness. Safe return doubtful." Destruction by ice entirely possible.

Now there is no reason to believe that Harriet Beecher Stowe was contemplating the climate of the poles in 1851 and 1852, when she began publishing her great antislavery novel, *Uncle Tom's Cabin*, in serial form. Yet it is tempting to wonder if the long search for the missing Franklin expedition may have inspired Stowe's most stirring scene. Sir John Franklin (known as "the man who ate his boots" in despair on a previous foray into the Arctic) had vanished, ships and all, in 1845 during a futile search for the Northwest Passage. Throughout the 1850s, the British Navy, along with various American rescue missions, combed the islands off the Canadian coast looking for survivors, without results. In 1852, a note found in a cairn strongly suggested that Franklin and his entire party had perished in the ice years earlier. The Franklin tragedy, as retailed in the nation's press, formed a kind of Greek chorus of danger and doom, setting the stage for Eliza's dramatic flight across the ice in Stowe's novel. This single scene, replayed on the stage for more than seventy-five years after the Civil War had ended, became an iconic episode in America's imaginative history. The floating ice on the Ohio River separates the young mulatto mother and her son from freedom, but it also provides the means of her deliverance from the hateful institution of slavery. Ice is danger and privation. Ice is liberation.

It all happens in two short paragraphs in chapter seven. Pursued by slave traders and a snarling pack of bloodhounds, Eliza hurls herself onto the river's ice floes, making for the State of Ohio, the antislavery North, and the Underground Railroad: "The huge green fragment of ice on which she alighted pitched and creaked. . . . With wild cries and desperate energy she leaped to another cake. . . . Blood marked every step." Stowe knew she had hit the right note of pathos and peril. "A thousand lives," she wrote, "seemed to be concentrated in that one moment to Eliza." But much of the incident came from newspaper reports of escapes by female slaves with babes in arms during the spring ice breakup on the Ohio River, including one highly publicized crossing to Ripley in 1838 (when Stowe was living in nearby Cincinnati).

Sales of her book were enormous—three hundred thousand copies during the first year after publication, second only to the Bible. *Uncle Tom's Cabin* was the best-selling novel of the nineteenth century. Scholars have discovered, moreover, that ten times the number of those 1852 readers (some three million people) saw stage versions of the story in the form of unauthorized "Tom" shows, which sprang up even while the book was still being serialized. These plays were typically wild-eyed melodramas and, depending on the intended audience's pro- or anti-abolitionist sentiments, vehicles for broad, comedic blackface minstrelsy. A 1906 *Billboard* magazine, in a brief history of "Tom" shows, maintained that the first New York City version opened in 1852 and managed to leave out the central characters of Topsy and Eva!

A more satisfactory adaptation was developed in November 1852 by the Howard family at their floating "museum" (a display of waxworks and curiosities where plays were also presented) in Troy, New York, as a vehicle for four-year-old Cordelia. Cordelia Howard, aka "The Youthful Wonder," was a hymn-singing prodigy who played the role of Little Eva. The hour-long Howard play, written by a cousin, soon moved to Gotham and eventually, under the aegis of P. T. Barnum, went to England. As Martin Scorsese showed in his own filmic chronicle of the era, *Gangs of New York* (2002), the play was a special favorite among the rough

New York crowd of Bowery b'hoys opposed to Lincoln and abolition. All-white casts of black slaves cavorted merrily to a musical score borrowed from Stephen Foster during the decade when the War Between the States turned comedy into tragedy.

After the Civil War, the dramatic version of *Uncle Tom's Cabin* became even more popular, although in Baltimore, Washington, and points south riots were liable to break out if the novel's antislavery bias was apparent. In the former Confederacy, "Tom" shows were acceptable only as comedic turns for "negro impersonators." Stetson, Peck, Conway, Rial, and Aiken are only a few of the impresarios/playwrights/companies who toured in tents, covered wagons, and railroad cars. The same amusement managers who booked the "Tom" shows also carried other attractions, like panorama paintings, for variety. One of the most popular and enduring panorama exhibitions playing alongside Stowe's stirring (or farcical) tale documented Elisha Kent Kane's 1855 expedition in search of Franklin and a mythical Open Polar Sea somewhere in the far North. Part and parcel with the giant, panoramic depiction of icebergs and snowfields came a team of real "esquimaux" dogs, an Inuit boy named Hans Christian, and, on occasion, Dr. Kane himself (the putative lover of spirit-rapping celebrity Margaret Fox).

By the turn of the century, "Tom" shows were still ubiquitous features of the small-town theatrical scene. Leon Washburn, a New York "general director" with offices on Broadway, was touring no fewer than four companies simultaneously, promising live field hands and dogs, a preshow parade, excellent stage machinery (treadmills to move the requisite ice floes), and, for even more fun and frolic, double or triple shows with multiple Toms and Topsys. Celebrities of the hour also appeared in lead roles, capitalizing on their off-stage fame. Prizefighter John L. Sullivan went on tour as Simon Legree in a company whose assets, costumes, and scenery were seized by angry creditors in 1902 in Waterbury, Connecticut. *Uncle Tom* barnstormed the country, setting up shop in tents, showboats, empty warehouses, and saloons. Every version, however abbreviated or embellished

Uncle Tom's Cabin poster, "Eliza's Escape," 1899

with showmanship, contained a few immutable scenes, including Eva's death, Tom's flogging, and, most important of all, Eliza's flight over the ice, the evening's dramatic highlight. A two-line review in a newspaper far from the bright lights of Broadway became a show-biz legend: *"Uncle Tom's Cabin* played here last night. The dogs were good."

But with competition from the movies and vaudeville, trade paper ads for new productions were soon crowded out by notices of "Tom" show backdrops, cabins, and properties on the block. "Will sell cheap for cash," wrote a New York lady in possession of a complete outfit. "Must go," tent and all, wrote a manager stranded in Sioux City, Iowa. Why travel to places even the circus dared not go when the Selig Polyscope Company was undercutting ticket prices with a sort of documentary photoplay of a "Tom" show parade for only a nickel a peep and a little cranking of a handle? By the 1930s, "Tom" shows had become a precious specimen of old-time Americana, alongside hand-sewn quilts and hand-carved

Anthony and Ellis poster, 1881

weathervanes. A Manhattan revival in 1933 attracted a flock of theatrical sophisticates, including Katharine Hepburn and Edna Ferber. According to a leading critic of the day, the production had the audience in tears as Eliza clutched her son and began her dash across the ice to freedom. Perhaps the tears were for the end of the barnstorming era.

Even Hollywood paid nostalgic tribute to the passing of the "Tom" show. *The Girl in the Show* (1929), starring Bessie Love, chronicled the vicissitudes of a cast of Evas and Elizas stranded in rural Kansas after the manager makes off with the box office receipts. The great D. W. Griffith, in search of an epic scene to enliven his film version of the old stage chestnut *Way Down East* (1920), was inspired to add a hair-raising Eliza chase—without hounds—relying on the moviegoer to recognize both the source and the symbolism. The ethereal Lillian Gish became the essence of wronged womanhood, pitted against the implacable coldness of ice floes tumbling down a New England river. The melodramatic poster shows her limp body dangling from the arms of co-star Richard Barthelmess, on the brink of an angry cataract bigger than Niagara Falls. Saved in the nick of time! But the grandest Eliza scene of them all was still to come, in director Harry A. Pollard's *Uncle Tom's Cabin* of 1927.

The project had personal significance for Pollard, a one-time actor who had played Tom in a road show and in a 1913 Universal film production. In addition, he also saw the story as a star vehicle for his wife, actress Margarita Fischer, then in semi-retirement. No matter that Fisher and her romantic lead were both white. The fact eased the studio's fears of a southern boycott, since the script was tailored to emphasize the familial love between George, Eliza, and their son rather than the nastier aspects of Tom's demise. But in other ways Pollard was a stickler for accuracy. Originally, he wanted to film the key ice scene on the Ohio River at Cairo, Illinois, near the locale described in Stowe's novel. When the weather failed to cooperate, he raced off to a rumored ice jam on the Allegheny at Franklin, Pennsylvania. Once again, Pollard was thwarted: nervous locals had prudently dynamited the ice. And so the cast and crew wound up on the Saranac River outside Plattsburgh, New York, in the grip of a terrible winter. At eleven o'clock in the morning, the temperature stood at -37 degrees. Pollard's teeth froze and broke in the bitter cold after he and Margarita were almost swept away by the river's current. Then came a blizzard.

For all their trials, however, the filming had not been completed by spring. In the end, the whole winter sequence had to be reshot on a studio back lot using water diverted from the Los Angeles River, fake ice floes tethered in place in the current, and artificial snow (cornflakes, gypsum, and salt). To simulate a blizzard's murky, misty air—with which Pollard was only too familiar—he burned two hundred tons of old tires, blanketing the city in acrid fumes for more than a month. When Pollard was done, he had created the equivalent of a modern-day blockbuster, one of the most expensive movies made to that date. Alas, the take barely equaled the expenses. Audiences were finally tired of Eliza and the ice—except in England, where a gala London premiere coaxed no less a figure than Josephine Baker to fly in from Paris.

There is no surer way to pinpoint the moment when a serious dramatic device becomes a stereotype than to note its casual use in the dime-store reaches of popular culture. While *Uncle Tom's Cabin* may have brought tears to the smart set's eyes in 1933, the familiar "Tom" show staging of the novel had already turned up in the 1932 movie *Spanky*. One of the "Our Gang" series of short comedies full of slapstick and irreverence, this was a film within a film, bracketing a backyard production of "Unkle Tom" between several showcase segments introducing the title character. The play portion is an exercise in juvenile ingenuity and mayhem, with "Stymie" playing dual parts as Tom and Topsy, adorable kids in blackface picking cotton while lip-synching spirituals to a record, Simon Legree under attack by a wrathful Eva, and a wonderful reprise of Eliza fleeing tipsily on a series of wooden crates roped together and vigorously jiggled by whatever actors are not currently onstage.

Because cartoons were not made exclusively for kids in the 1920s and '30s, Walt Disney's *Mickey's Mellerdrammer* (1933) expects the audience to understand its sly reuse of stereotypes, from an Al Jolson spoof to a detailed send-up of the "Tom" shows, with their peculiar mixture of serious subject matter, high drama, and black caricature. Act two, scene three—the homemade let's-have-a-play—is another Eliza escape with the lead role taken by Clarabelle Cow, one of the Disney stock company of barnyard stars. The fake ice cakes are mounted on a treadmill powered by a bicycle. Sound effects consist of potatoes dropping on a tin pan. The backdrop is a panorama laced together with seams of string. And poor Eliza is being chased by a pack of stray dogs outfitted in little bloodhound suits. When Mickey, as Tom/Topsy, mistakenly zips a cat into one of the dog costumes, it escapes, lands on Eliza's head, and sends the "bloodhounds" charging into the orchestra pit, ending the play in utter chaos.

Cartoons like this one, and Tex Avery's 1937 and 1947 versions of Pollard's film, were something of an embarrassment to the industry after animation became the mainstay of children's television in the 1950s. Avery's Warner Bros. titles were among the "Censored 11" banned from the small screen after they were acquired by Ted Turner. *Mickey's Mellerdrammer* has only recently been rescued from obscurity on a limited-edition DVD introduced by Leonard Maltin with an apologia for the media's use of racial stereotypes in a less-enlightened past. He does not mention the splendid irony of Mickey, Minnie, and the gang "blacking up" when they were, in fact, the most revered black actors of their age.

Yet it was during the 1950s, when the nation's segregationist history came under direct challenge, that one of the most enduring and beloved dramas in the American theater chose to reinvigorate both the racial issues inherent in Stowe's book and the tradition of the "Tom" show. *The King and I,* the Rodgers and Hammerstein musical which opened on Broadway in 1951, did so with charm and verve, thanks to the performances of Yul Brynner as the king and Gertrude Lawrence as Anna, the British widow hired to instruct the royal children of exotic Siam. The surprise centerpiece of the production—a play within a play—was a song-and-dance version of a "Tom" show, performed in Siamese masks and whiteface. This was the pivot on which the plot turned. Could, would the despotic king set his beautiful slave free? Would his fascination with the Bible and with President Abraham Lincoln help him to adopt Stowe's abolitionist point of view? Can the teacher "modernize" Siam and its monarchy without destroying both?

Whether the story is true or not seems to bother many students of the theater. The plot came from a book written by the real Anna Leonowens about her experiences in Bangkok in the early 1860s. Her memoir formed the basis for a 1944 novel by Margaret Landon—*Anna and the King of Siam*—and the script for a 1946 nonmusical film of the same name starring a mannered and somewhat twitchy Rex Harrison. Here, in grainy black and white, the play staged by the court is a brief history of Siam. The real genius of the splashy Rodgers and Hammerstein version is the decision to place *Uncle Tom's Cabin* at the heart of the plot and to present it as a classical "Tom" show called "Small House of Uncle Thomas," with choreography by Jerome Robbins.

The King and I, in its big-screen, DeLuxe color, Cinema-Scope incarnation of 1956, preserves the Robbins staging and may even improve upon it by the forceful contrast between the orientalized abstraction of the darkened stage and

"Small House of Uncle Thomas Ballet," from *The King and I*

the quick reaction shots of the audience seated in a bright, opulent ballroom. Every pivotal scene in the movie, from the King's letter to Lincoln offering a gift of elephants to his inner conflict over punishing a runaway slave, refers back to the "Tom" show, whose author and narrator is the beautiful and seditious concubine, Lady Tuptin. And so the performance becomes an allegory of life in the kingdom, with Eliza standing for Tuptin as she flees "King Simon of Legree" across the faraway realm of Kentucky. The obstacles she encounters in her balletic escape are represented by fluttering scarves: blue for rain, green for mountains, and, finally, white for the waters of the "O-hee-o" River. But wherever she goes, Legree follows with his snarling pack of "scientific dogs" sniffing at her heels. In the end, it is prayer that saves Eliza, as Buddha (mounted on the top of a sort of Jacob's ladder) sends his angel to freeze the ice so she can cross—and to melt it again, drowning Legree and his companions. The scenario, in other words, conflates the biblical story of Moses crossing the Nile out of Egypt with Stowe's story of Eliza's escape across the ice. On the stage, at any rate, the King/Legree/Pharaoh perishes for his sins—a Negro spiritual with a Thai twist. The Old Testamental parallels embedded in *Uncle Tom's Cabin* are revealed and emphasized.

South Pacific, a few years earlier, had broached the subject of prejudice in the context of a culture clash between an American naval unit occupying an idyllic island inhabited by French colonists and native peoples. *The King and I* returned to the theme with a Cold War emphasis on harmony among nations and races. But the "Tom" show not only addressed internationalism but also international perceptions of the mounting civil rights movement at home as well as the nation's historic conflict over a problem that even the Civil War and Harriet Beecher Stowe had proved powerless to solve. Just as the original "Tom" shows faced rioting in the American South, producers feared that their big-budget movie might inflame viewers in contemporary Dixie. Black actress Dorothy Dandridge, fresh from her triumph in *Carmen Jones*, turned down the role of Tuptin when she learned of the "Tom" show scene. But the lively score, the dazzling costumes, and the sheer romance of the film sugarcoated its liberalism, even in the South. *The King and I* passed for the kind of harmless, cultural do-goodism purveyed by the State Department in the aftermath of World War II.

> Walt Disney's *Bambi* (1942) contains one of **HOLLY-WOOD'S BEST ICE SCENES**. The story takes its structure from the cycle of the seasons. In the winter scene, Thumper (a bunny) teaches an awkward Bambi (a fawn) how to skate on the mysterious hard water.

The use of ice as the medium of deliverance in *The King and I* is particularly miraculous because the players and their monarch are clearly unacquainted with the properties of "hard water." Ice redeems because it is a gift from heaven and the Buddha, like the manna in the wilderness God sent to the followers of Moses. This salvific baptism by ice is one of the major motifs in what may be America's favorite Christmas movie, *It's a Wonderful Life*. Made in 1946, in the same period of postwar reflection and exuberance that influenced the musicals of Rodgers and Hammerstein, Frank Capra's film revolves around the motifs of fall and rescue. The key scene has a despairing George

Bailey (Jimmy Stewart) about to throw himself into the ice-choked waters of a river. But by rescuing his guardian angel, Clarence, from the ice floes, George eventually saves himself. The incident on the river, meanwhile, recapitulates a pivotal moment in George's childhood when he saved his younger brother from drowning beneath the ice of a skating pond. That act set the tone for an adult life of service to the town of Bedford Falls. Even his romance and eventual marriage are conceptually related to these "accidents": George falls for his future wife when the pair accidentally plunge together into the placid waters of the high school pool. Ice represents crisis, pain, and a hard-won salvation. Water without ice is a benign baptism.

> There are several American figures called **THE ICEMAN**. One is New Jersey multiple murderer Richard Kuklinski, who claims to have killed more than two hundred people, storing their bodies in the freezer vault of a Mister Softee ice cream truck. **THE ICEMAN** of Marvel Comics fame is a teenager who can freeze the moisture in the air around him into super-hard ice. Although he was known as **ICE MAN** over a long career, Terry Labonte, once a favorite on the NASCAR circuit, actually preferred Marvel's Spiderman.

Cold-weather towns in upstate New York have squabbled for decades over which of them was the "real" Bedford Falls. Was it Utica? Troy? Seneca Falls? But unlike Pollard, who had dragged his crew across half a continent in search of genuine ice, Capra settled for the back lot and Encino, California. The irony in Capra's choice of location revealed itself in 1992, when a low-budget teen comedy—*Encino*

Man—was released in Europe. The storyline has a pair of high school stoners improbably digging up a block of ice in the sandy expanse of a local backyard. And from that block (which seems impervious to the heat of a California day) emerges a prehistoric teenager, an Ice Age cave-stoner who manages to fit in perfectly at the local senior high. Now a cult favorite, *Encino Man* has its moments as a spoof of California pop culture and Hollywood movies in which monsters ranging from Frankenstein's creature to The Thing arise from the ice to menace civilization. Ah, the horror of it all! Ah, Encino!

> In the 1880s, the wife of a millionaire California senator had her lawns covered in **CRUSHED ICE** to amuse a houseguest from Vermont on Christmas morning.

The movie business may be fascinated with ice that doesn't come in cocktail glasses because it is utterly foreign to Southern California—and therefore rare, exotic, and desirable. Movie starlets revel in fur coats and warm sheepskin booties from Australia. Despite the messiness of cornflake snow, Hollywood seems drawn to the chill of northern locations, especially for Christmas stories that are supposed to look like Hallmark scenes of ice-bound Vermont. Based on an earlier film (*Holiday Inn*, 1942) and even earlier musical numbers by Irving Berlin, *White Christmas* (1954) was another of the decade's big, showy, colorful, must-see VistaVision extravaganzas. The setting is Vermont in the dead of a snowless winter. The cold of the outdoors sets up a contrast with the warm interior of a failing country inn. The proprietor, the general, is Bing Crosby's World War II commander, and Bing, with the help of his friends, sets out to save the inn by mounting a show.

So far, *White Christmas* could be a Judy Garland/ Mickey Rooney flick with some grown-up hanky-panky. But the addition of a number left over from the previous film and staged with the élan of "Small House of Uncle Thomas" changes the picture. The number is "Abraham," and it was filmed as classical minstrelsy, with Rosemary Clooney, Bing Crosby, and the chorus acting the parts of the interlocutor and the "end men," Tambo and Bones. In other words, without a compelling justification for doing so in the script, *White Christmas* manages to brew up a hot toddy of civil rights, the Bible, the Negro spiritual, patriotism, Santa Claus, and a hint of the old "Tom" show. It is probably fitting that as the last song is sung, snow begins to fall outside the inn. All is well inside, un-cold, no ice. Merry Christmas!

In Canto 32 of his *Inferno*, the thirteenth-century Florentine poet Dante Alighieri, in the company of the Roman poet Virgil, descends into the lowest circle of a conical hell, deep beneath the surface of the earth. There, in the very pit of damnation, he encounters not the expected fire but ice—the ice of lovelessness. And there, in a huge frozen lake, Dante finds the assigned resting place for traitors and the lair of Satan himself, "where all the weight of everything bears down." The Dark One is frozen into the center of the lake, condemned to beat his great bat's wings in helpless fury forever. His flapping creates the wind known as Cocytus, the icy breath of all evil. The more Satan flails, the thicker grows his ice prison. The world, it seems, has ended not in fire after all but in the ice on which Stowe's brave Eliza, driven by love for her son, escaped the hell of slavery.

Ice-Skating

American artist Joseph Cornell added a famous legend to the history of ice in 1940 with a small box titled "Taglioni's Jewel Casket" (MoMA). According to the story pasted inside the lid, the nineteenth-century ballerina Marie Taglioni, renowned for being the first to dance *en pointe* without the aid of hoisting apparatus, was seized by a highwayman one cold Russian night. In return for her freedom, he demanded that she dance for him alone on a panther skin spread over the ice of the steppes. She treasured the memory of the fantastic and romantic moment and, ever afterward, carried a cube of artificial ice in her jewelry box. (Cornell gave her enough cubes to chill a large vodka and tonic!) This celebrated event makes Marie Taglioni the first **FIGURE SKATER.**

Modern figure skating is a perplexing mixture of athletics and artistry, sport and entertainment. The 1994 attack on Nancy Kerrigan orchestrated by rival Tonya Harding shows how, whatever it may be, figure skating has become a fixture of celebrity culture. One of the earliest

Silver Skates Derby, Minneapolis, 1936

ice shows, headlined by German ice ballerina Charlotte Oelschlagel, was imported from Berlin in 1915 and performed at the New York City Hippodrome. A true sensation, the show ran for three hundred days. A silent movie, *The Frozen Warning* (1916), the first film built around figure skating, was based on the Oelschlagel performance. In the ensuing decades, ice-skaters rapidly became entertainers—and movie stars.

> **ARTIFICIAL ICE-SKATING RINKS** made of interlocking panels of a polymer compound can be assembled in minutes in any climate for figure skating shows and practice rinks. Silicone is often applied to skates and the "ice" surface to enhance the "glide effect."

Norwegian Olympic champion Sonja Henie was a major force in Hollywood in the 1930s; her skating movies were the box office sensations of the Depression years. Walt Disney spoofed Henie's films in 1939 with a Donald Duck short in which the hero appears bedecked with Sonja's long eyelashes and short, tight curls. In *The Ice Follies of 1939*, aimed at stealing Henie's limelight, Joan Crawford played a skating star in a "B" production saved from mediocrity by a Technicolor ice show tacked on at the end and starring the cast of the Ice Follies.

A traveling live show, the Ice Follies had been launched in 1936–37 by champions Roy and Eddie Shipstad and Oscar Johnson in St. Paul, Minnesota, to take advantage of skating stars' newfound popularity. One feature of the Shipstad-Johnson show was the inclusion of comic and novelty acts, like Frick and Frack. Ice Capades was founded in 1940 in Hershey, Pennsylvania, by John Harris, who had noted a rise in attendance at the hockey games he promoted when he booked Sonja Henie for a half-time show. Disney on Ice, owned by the same firm that produces the Ringling Bros. Circus, is a more recent entry into the ice show business, along with a number of touring companies organized around the routines of medal-winning competitive skaters.

Oscar Johnson and Eddie Shipstad in the Ice Follies, 1938

What would an ice show or a hockey game be without a **ZAMBONI?** The motorized ice groomer was born in Southern California in 1939. Frank Zamboni and his family, taking advantage of an ice-skating craze, opened a rink—"Iceland"—in the town of Paramount. Searching for a way to keep the surface smooth and flat, he tinkered with a combination of tractors, shaving blades, and hot water tanks and in 1949 applied for a patent. His second sale was to Sonja Henie, then touring in her own "Hollywood on Ice Review." The fourth unit went to the Ice Capades in 1952 and is now in the collection of the U.S. Hockey Hall of Fame in Eveleth, Minnesota. In many arenas, the Zamboni driver is a local celebrity. And spectators sing the Zamboni song, recorded in Austin, Minnesota, by a local band called the Gear Daddies.

Blades of Glory (2007), a comedy with Will Ferrell and Jon Heder as the world's first male pairs skaters, satirizes the soap-opera emotionalism, the cheesy costumes, and the preposterous choreography of Olympic-level figure skating and arena ice shows. In *Hannah and Her Sisters* (1986), Woody Allen speculates on the Nietzschean concept of eternal recurrence. "He said that the life we lived we're going to live over again the exact same way for eternity," Allen laments. "Great. That means I'll have to sit through the Ice Capades again."

Meanwhile, Minnesota's Mall of America has been wooing the failing World Figure Skating Museum and Hall of Fame of Colorado Springs (once located in Boston), with its collection of competition records, medals, costumes, skates, and Sonja Henie films.

3

ROMANTIC ICE

"I seek the everlasting ices of the north"

—

Mary Shelley, *Frankenstein* (1818)

 On April 24, 1861, twelve days after the Civil War began with the Confederate attack on Fort Sumter, Frederic Church advised the public that his latest "Great Picture" was ready for viewing at Goupil's New York showrooms. The "Great Picture"— a huge canvas full of detail and current interest—was the entrepreneurial Church's specialty. The work in question was advertised in planted "news" stories hinting at a never-before-seen sight in the offing. And the painting, when finally unveiled, was displayed in a controlled setting with real props and foliage, elaborate framing mechanisms, and a programme or booklet calling attention to the image's more remarkable features. Of course, the art lover paid admission to the spectacle—twenty-five cents in the case of Church's 5.5 by 9.5–foot *The Icebergs*.

While the gallery hoopla was in progress, the artist and his agent were busily arranging the next stops on an extended tour. Boston, with its snooty sense of being America's aesthetic center, was always on the itinerary. But so was London, where the world's best color lithographers could be engaged to produce the prints that were the major profit center of the art business. In the meantime, behind the scenes, the wheels of commerce kept turning. Were any potential buyers for the original in sight? It was all the better, of course, if that patron of the arts was a famous personage.

The Civil War, however, threatened to bring the whole, well-oiled system to a shuddering halt. Church countered by renaming his work *The North! A Picture of Icebergs!* thereby subtly affirming his allegiance to the Union cause. If it quietly became *The Icebergs* once more in the summer of 1863 when the road show opened in London, nobody there took notice. Mercantile Britain, with strong interests in the American cotton trade, was rumored to be on the verge of openly favoring the Confederacy. Fortunately for Church, though, his subject matter tapped into a deeper wellspring of sentiment surrounding the glories and tragedies of Arctic exploration, in which the British had taken a leading role throughout the nineteenth century.

Lady Franklin, the feisty wife of Sir John—leader of the lost Franklin expedition of 1845 in search of the Northwest Passage—and many of those who led the forty-odd search parties looking for him, attended a preview, along with a host of glacier experts, geographers, and royals. In a way, the exhibition of *The Icebergs* marked the end of the long hunt for Franklin and his crew of 139. No less a figure than Charles Dickens had appeared in a Franklin-inspired

play called *The Frozen Deep* in 1857. A somber monument
to Franklin, replete with sculpted bergs, was dedicated in
Greenwich in 1859. Since a shattered ship's mast forming
a kind of cruciform memorial was added to *The Icebergs*
shortly before the London showing, it is probable that
Church himself intended to pay tribute to John Franklin
(and potential English purchasers). The picture was a last,
sad, calculated good-bye, overlaid with religious sentiment.

Throughout the 1850s, Americans were caught up in the
drama and mystery of Franklin's disappearance (the first relics only came to light in 1854) and in the lure of the Arctic.
There was glory and national honor to be won on the polar
ice. American explorers like Elisha Kent Kane combed the
north for signs of the vanished command. Dr. Isaac Hayes,
ship's surgeon on one of Kane's voyages, was a friend of
Frederic Church and a fervent believer in an "Open Polar
Sea" lying beyond the barrier of icebergs that blocked the
route to this fantastic and magic place. A riveting platform
speaker, Hayes also appealed to national pride in calling on
Americans to get there first, to claim the Frozen North for
their own. His heady brew of exoticism, the great unknown,
a little science, and the chilling heroics of the British were
enough to rouse his countrymen's interest. Manifest Destiny
at the roof of the world! Unsurpassed beauty! Coleridge's
"Rime of the Ancient Mariner" come to life, in all its wonder
and terror! Above all, the great, mysterious, and beautiful
icebergs: "And ice, mast-high, came floating by / As green as
emerald," wrote the poet, imagining these majestic travelers
of the north. So it was that Church, in the company of the
Reverend Louis Noble, set sail from Boston in the spring of
1859 bound for the North Atlantic, Labrador, and the bergs.

Noble, the biographer of Church's teacher Thomas Cole, acted as official historian of the adventure. Fond of the Bible, poetry, and Church in roughly equal measure, Noble's real task was to publish a book about the painter among the icebergs meant to rouse interest in the monumental painting to come. Church's exquisite pencil sketches of the icebergs the pair encountered, in their modesty and verisimilitude, give little hint of the finished work shown to almost universal acclaim on Broadway nearly three years later. It is not simply that the painting is so big that the viewer seems to be standing in the scene, on the shelf of ice in the foreground. Indeed, the souvenir guidebook (probably written by Church) specifies that the "beholder" is situated on the edge of a bay carved out of an enormous berg, lost in the elements: "Waves and currents, sunshine and storms." But the painting is more than an inventory of the tricky, natural effects of sky, water, and reflection that Church and Noble recorded in Labrador.

Frederic Edwin Church, *The Icebergs*, 1861

It is dazzling in color and light and more than a little eerie, full of a kind of sublime spookiness left over from the Romanticism of a previous era. The ice cliff on the left resolves itself into grotesque faces—and a nude female body—fantastically embedded in a frozen matrix of violent blues and greens. On the right, an ice cavern of a poisonous emerald hue leads to an unimaginable noplace. Church's painting manages to be ominous, gorgeous, and unaccountable all at the same time, with a gleam of mad obsession lingering beneath every brushstroke. In a way, the addition of the Christian cross—the mast of a sunken ship—seems too literal, too mundane an intrusion into the gelid, haunted waters off the great Humboldt Glacier.

The British critic John Ruskin, that stalwart champion of J. M. W. Turner's maelstroms of the north, was not bedazzled by the Church, although the latter specialized in the closely observed detail Ruskin wrote about. Nor was Ruskin impressed with the appended cross, even as he compared the Alps to Gothic cathedrals in rapturous prose. The reason, perhaps, was that disquieting sense of the freakish, the inexplicable, the malevolent that lurks behind Church's sunshiny Arctic cove. Behind the optimism of Manifest Destiny, behind the plucky hucksterism of the American salesman, this remains a place of nameless horror. Potential buyers may have felt disquieted in the presence of Church's grand vision, too. Although the chromolithographs by Charles Risdon sold briskly enough, the canvas was not disposed of immediately. It was only in 1865 that it was sold to a British Member of Parliament and investor in Canadian railroads (which, he said, would solve the problem of a Northwest Passage in a thoroughly modern way). The buyer bought the work on a trip to New York and shipped it back to his country estate near Manchester, where it vanished from the record until 1979.

Sir Edward Watkin, otherwise known as the "Railway King," was not an unknown personage in the world of Anglo-American art and commerce. Nor was he insensitive to the wilder aspects of nature. According to his journal for 1861, he had viewed an iceberg firsthand from the deck of a ship bound for Canada. It was, he said, an object of a "fairy-like whiteness . . . which was very beautiful to see." As he stood there mesmerized, "a great mass broke away, toppled over into the sea, sending up an immense snowy spray, and disappeared." Ethereal but real. And gone in an instant, like a ghost. A man of taste who mingled with the luminaries of the world of nineteenth-century culture, including Henry Wadsworth Longfellow, William Cullen Bryant, Robert Browning, and Charles Dickens, Watkin found something in Church's chilling visual poetry that reminded him of his own imaginings.

Icebound in Lake Superior, 1880

Ice—the sublime fury of the North—roused the curiosity of even homebound Europeans. Ruskin made three difficult trips into the Alps between the 1830s and 1866, observing glaciers in the teeth of a blizzard and concluding that the howling winds gave the scene "the appearance of a vast Polar sea." The German painter Caspar David Friedrich helped to create a quasi-religious cult of the North as a symbol of purity and faith. But mysticism turned to despair. *The Sea of Ice* (1823–24), his late, dismal vision of jagged pressure ridges thrusting knifelike points of ice high into the sky, was once called "The Wreck of [the] *Hope*" after a fragment of a ship being pressed into oblivion by the restless action of the sea. "Abandon hope all ye who enter here!" is the warning Dante inscribes above the Gates of Hell. Ice is hell.

In many parts of the world, human bodies in remarkable states of preservation have been found in cold places, often at high altitudes. These include the "Ice Maiden of the Andes," discovered in 1995, the 2,400-year-old Siberian ice maiden (1993), and "Otzi," the 5,300-year-old hunter/shepherd found by a mountaineer in the Alps in 1991. Similar remains, later cremated and buried, were found in the Yukon in 1999. Some of these ICE MUMMIES were treated with desiccants shortly after death, but in all cases ice was the main reason for their intact state. Scientists stand to learn a great deal about ancient agriculture, ritual, and physical development from examination of these corpses.

For the nineteenth century, ice could stand for a miraculous rebirth of feeling, a lonely, silent death, or, in the hands of the American painter William Bradford, the triumph of science and enterprise. During nine voyages above the Arctic Circle, he painted moderately sized views of icebergs, glaciers, and the frozen sea. In 1869, however, inspired by Noble's book, he documented his trek to Greenland with 141 albumen prints, published under the title *The Arctic Regions*. Whether Bradford actually made some of the stunning photos of his ship "nipped" in the ice or not, he certainly organized and directed the work of the two professional photographers aboard. Science, hope, and danger met on the ice fields of Melville Bay.

The Bradford photographs bear descriptive titles intended to speak to his readership in terms they would understand. A partial view of the ship's masts and a small boat's prow beset in a crowded ice field, for example, is labeled *Here We Were Surrounded by the Wildest Scene Possible to Conceive*. What is ice? What is the Arctic? Wild beyond all imagining—a challenge, a vision so terrible as not to be believed without photographic evidence. In the 1850s and '60s, ice was a suitable symbol in America for a natural awfulness that instantly summoned up its opposite human virtues—fortitude, heroism, and grace.

Bradford, Dunmore, and Critcherson, "Here We Were Surrounded by the Wildest Scene Possible to Conceive," *The Arctic Regions*, 1869

Landscape photographer Craig Blacklock of Moose Lake, Minnesota—best known for his shots of the North Shore—took a new direction in a spectacular book and exhibition entitled *A Voice Within: The Lake Superior Nudes* (2004). This project daringly juxtaposes the nude body of his wife with the rocky coastline. The most challenging and problematic of these images capture **HONEY BLACKLOCK STRETCHED OUT ON A BED OF SHATTERED SHORE ICE** or within a towering cave guarded by icicles taller than she. The pictures set up a tense dialogue between human fragility and nature's forces, between sensuality and indifference in a cold place where Venus does not often rise from the frozen sea.

Emanuel Leutze, the German American history painter, produced several versions of *Washington Crossing the Delaware* at midcentury. The subject matter, drawn from the American Revolution, also alluded to European revolutions of 1848. But Americans saw the work as a cornerstone of their own epochal past. More than fifty thousand people came to see the picture in New York in October 1851. In Washington, DC, the tumult was even greater. Before a collector snapped up Leutze's masterpiece, Congress, notoriously gun-shy about matters of taste, discussed buying it for the White House.

During the 1930s, as the bicentennial of Washington's birth approached, critics took a second look at *Crossing the Delaware*. By then, it had become an icon of Americanism, displayed in sepia prints in schoolrooms, courthouses, and government offices. But a new wave of nitpickers was troubled by the enormous crags and pinnacles of ice that crowded Leutze's view of the placid Delaware River (which the artist actually modeled on C. D. Friedrich and the

Rhine). The strongest objection came to the figure of Washington standing up in the boat. Debunkers insisted that on a stormy December night, the sensible Father of His Country would have done no such thing.

Yet the glory of *Washington Crossing the Delaware* is in the contrast between the calm fortitude of the hero and the turbulent, disordered tumble of ice floes below him. Whether the living Washington ever did pose in this fashion or not is profoundly beside the point. The ice stands for every awful obstacle to freedom and to life. Given the outpouring of interest in the painting in 1851, on the seventy-fifth anniversary of the event, it is not altogether surprising that Harriet Beecher Stowe, in the same year, staged Eliza's melodramatic flight to freedom on Leutze's ice floes.

In England, where a cult of ice was already full blown, the Romantic poets were particularly susceptible to the wilder, quasi-mystical aspects of the winter landscape. Shortly after sending his Ancient Mariner into the Antarctic Sea, Samuel Taylor Coleridge himself visited a frozen lake in Germany and wrote at length about its mysteries: its many colors, he argued, showed that the frozen ice was alive and animate, the mystical complement to the sunlit pleasure domes of his own "Kubla Khan" (1798). In 1816, Percy Shelley made a literary pilgrimage to Chamonix, beneath the frozen abysses of Mount Blanc, in search of similar enlightenment. He was accompanied on his travels by his teenage mistress (and soon-to-be wife) Mary Godwin, a writer herself, who had heard Coleridge recite the "Rime" in her parents' parlor.

Eventually, the Shelleys fetched up at Lord Byron's Villa Diodati in Switzerland, where, kept indoors by incessant rain, they proposed a literary contest. Who could write the

Emanuel Leutze, *Washington Crossing the Delaware*, 1851

best ghost story, suitable for reading on dark, damp alpine nights? Over the course of the next several years, the other guests dropped out. Despite the death of a daughter and the birth of a son, Mary kept at it. Meanwhile, the world began to ponder the ice that lay within sight of the villa. A widely read treatise called *The Polar Ice* (1817), published by an Arctic whaler, put forth the case that the ice cap was thinning out for the first time in fifty years, and British officials, energized by the report, proposed voyages to locate the North Pole and the elusive Northwest Passage. With the Napoleonic Wars over, the admiralty seized on a quest for the pole as a means of employing its idle ships and naval officers. And Mary Wollstonecraft Godwin Shelley, back in London in the midst of the discussion, published *Franken-stein; or, The Modern Prometheus* anonymously in 1818.

Today, the word *Frankenstein* conjures up childhood memories of Boris Karloff's lurching, black-and-white movie monster (1931), with his square forehead and a pair of metal bolts through his neck—or a cinematic sequel, adaptation, or parody. For all intents and purposes, Frankenstein is the creature and not the creator. It is all just another horror story, an antique, sci-fi version of a Stephen King bestseller. Mary Shelley's name is not a household word, either: in the early nineteenth century, the book was often attributed to her husband. What everybody remembers best is the lightning, the primitive machinery, and a hunchback named Igor—Hollywood inventions nowhere to be found in the story. What nobody remembers is the fact

Boris Karloff as Frankenstein's monster, 1931

that *Frankenstein* begins and ends on the ice of the North Pole, where the maker dies and his handiwork consigns himself to a Viking funeral on an ice raft adrift in the polar sea. "He was soon borne away by the waves," reads the last line of Mary Shelley's masterpiece, "and lost in darkness and distance."

In its own day, *Frankenstein* was taken in some quarters for a philosophic contribution to the public discussion of Arctic exploration. John Wilson Croker, first lord of the admiralty—the man then in charge of mounting polar expeditions—panned the book in *The Quarterly Review* in January 1818. Of especial repugnance to Croker was the depiction of the Arctic as a place where men might readily be driven mad by sheer horror and the rigor of the elements. British explorers, he acidly remarked, "had not yet enlightened mankind upon the *real* state of the North Pole." The scene aboard the icebound ship where Frankenstein dies and the creature escapes into the desolate reaches of eternal cold was "a tissue of horrible and disgusting absurdity."

Did Croker sense an undercurrent of anti-imperialism in Shelley's decision to make her driven sea captain/explorer abandon the hunt for the pole after his strange encounters? Yet this age was one of curiosity and speculation. The ambitious Captain Walton has come in search of glory and the secrets of the universe, much as the young Dr. Victor Frankenstein goes off to the university at Ingolstadt to find the secret of life itself in the study of natural philosophy. Indeed, *The Quarterly Review,* in the years shortly before Mary Shelley's novel saw the light of day, had issued reports on subjects ranging from polar exploration and electricity to vivisection and the first stirrings of speculation on evolution. Along with Goethe (the monster learns to read from a text of *The Sorrows of Young Werther*), Milton, Dante, and Coleridge, she makes repeated allusions to contemporary science in Victor's deathbed recollection of his quest to create life. Born in an atmosphere of scientific inquiry, then, *Frankenstein* imagines the logical and horrific consequences of possibility unchecked by humility and forethought.

> Maurice Sendak's *Outside Over There* (1981) is the strange, scary, surreal story of a family saddened by Father's absence at sea. While Mother weeps by the shore, Sister Ida allows the baby to be stolen away by goblins in search of a bride. The goblins leave behind A HORRID ICE BABY, which promptly melts away. Ida bravely rescues her sister, Mother receives a letter from Father, and all ends well.

One of the themes shared by author and novel is childbirth. Frankenstein's mother dies in labor as he resumes his studies, bent on creating life like a new God. Mary Shelley's mother also died in childbirth, and the author herself gave birth to four children between 1815 and 1819, of whom only one survived. The secrets of life and death and the agonies of flesh form the background to Mary's harrowing story of arrogance gone mad and ego triumphing over love. The ice, the cold, the emptiness, the deaths of her protagonists signal the death of human warmth, the perils of thought over feeling. And even as she finished her great imaginative summary of the dangers and glories of her lifetime, England sent out the first of its great national missions to the ice fields: Buchan and Ross in 1818, Barrow in 1819, Franklin's first expedition and Parry in 1819, and Ross again in 1829. In 1831, while Ross and his nephew were still trapped in the ice after discovering the magnetic North Pole, the second edition of *Frankenstein* was published.

When Sir John Franklin set off to find the Northwest Passage, his may have been the best-appointed polar expedition ever assembled in the history of the British Navy. In addition to the tins of goods, the tents, and the other provisions for bodily comfort, Franklin sailed with a trunk of costumes for midwinter theatricals and a substantial library which seems to have included Mary Shelley's *Frankenstein,* the first novel to make use of published accounts of Arctic exploration. The fantasy that Croker railed against in 1818 had become uncanny truth for the *Erebus* and the *Terror* in 1845. The ships simply sailed into oblivion, "lost in darkness and distance." Franklin's faithful wife, Jane, held out hope for his return, fending off charges of cannibalism among the crew until 1859, when the relief ship *Fox* returned to England with the contents of the expedition's last cairn (three Franklin graves were only located in 1984).

But the mysterious disappearance and apparent obliteration of the lost Franklin expedition continued to nettle national pride. In 1874, John Everett Millais's *The North-west Passage,* a painting subtitled "It might be done and England should do it," caused a sensation at the annual Royal Academy spring exhibition because it seemed to insist that the quest for a sea route to Asia should not be abandoned on account of the Franklin tragedy. The picture shows a fierce old sea dog seated at a table topped with a map of the far North. Behind him, on the wall, hang a portrait of Nelson and a scene of a ship trapped in a frozen wasteland. Outside the window, a placid ocean. Inside, a brace of battle flags from warships of long ago. In the foreground, a solemn young woman (impersonated by Mrs. Millais) reads aloud from a tattered logbook. The implication is clear: Britain must lead the way through the passage to empire!

The crusty old gentleman who sat for Millais was "Captain" Edward Trelawny, sometimes described as an adventurer—or an outright charlatan. Certainly he had led a colorful and rackety life, including a stint as a volunteer alongside Lord Byron in the Greek wars of independence. But his pertinence to the Romantic view of the North Pole comes in his personal attachment to Byron and the Shelleys. Trelawny was in Italy in 1822, on terms of some intimacy with the Shelley ménage. It was he who brought Mary the news of her husband's death in a shipwreck, he who took

Sir John Everett Millais, *The North-west Passage*, 1874

charge of the cremation of the body on the beach where it had washed ashore, and he who plucked the poet's unburned heart from the ashes. When Trelawny died in 1881, his housekeeper took his ashes to Rome and buried them next to Shelley, in a plot her master had bought in 1822.

Old age had made Trelawny famously crabby; he was especially nettled by the fact that Sir John had placed a tumblerful of brandy—or rum—at his right hand in the painting. Strong drink aside, however, Millais sees him, with some degree of accuracy, lost in the memory of Britain's seafaring past but angrily insisting on the ultimate success of her efforts in the conquest of the North. Victor Frankenstein believed he could defeat death through reason and science. Trelawny here insists that courage and experience will win the day.

The North-west Passage did not inspire the Royal Navy and the Royal Geographical Society to complete Franklin's mission; that would be accomplished by Fridtjof Nansen, a Norwegian, in 1896. Instead, England began a quixotic assault on the North Pole. In 1875, a British Arctic Expedition officially embarked on that meaningless enterprise, under the leadership of Captain George Nares. In effect, this was another hunt for Franklin; Nares was directed to leave messages for the missing in cairns along the way and Lady Franklin's plucky motto "Hold Fast!" was emblazoned on the backs of the men charged with hauling the sleds over the ice to the pole. But Nares and his ships were back in Portsmouth in 1876, defeated by an outbreak of scurvy. Science had failed them. Well into the twentieth century, Arctic and Antarctic explorers would die terrible deaths in the ice and snow, crippled by pains in the legs, swelling, and a debilitating tiredness. Starved for the as-yet-undiscovered vitamin C, they went forth onto the ice and were "lost in darkness" forever, like Frankenstein's monster.

> One of ice's many uses before embalming became commonplace in the mid-nineteenth century was the temporary preservation of corpses to allow time for proper funeral rituals. More common, however, was the use of a plain, iceless plank called a **"COOLING BOARD."** A witness to the aftermath of Abraham Lincoln's assassination reported that his remains were taken out of the box "in which they were enclosed, all limp and warm," laid out on the floor, and "then stretched upon the cooling board." In most cases, however, with burial expected on the day after death, the board simply provided a place for the deceased to reside as the coffin was being made. In the South, where lots of ice would seem to be called for, the body sometimes rested on the board for three full days—a kind of insurance against premature burial. Only when that space of time had passed was death pronounced and the remains readied for the tomb. In the North, the dearly departed was bound to the board and stood upright in the barn during cold winters when it was impossible to dig a grave.

Although film versions of *Frankenstein* established an iconographic vocabulary for telling the story, they have varied widely in quality and intent. The Boris Karloff classic of 1931 sticks to alpine scenery and omits any reference to polar wastelands. A very British straight-to-TV film, subtitled "The True Story" (1973), was coauthored by Christopher Isherwood. It opens with a kind of prelude showing Victor and a sinking ship adrift amid crashing icebergs but is otherwise all Regency glamour, visual allusions to ice (in the

The Snowmobile

The **SNOWMOBILE** has many proud fathers. Virtually every firm producing these workhorses of ice country claims to be the very first. Minnesota, Wisconsin, Saskatchewan, and Quebec number among the cold-weather spots that insist upon their primacy. Admiral Byrd took an auto-conversion snowmobile to the South Pole in 1931. Although it failed to perform as promised, makers B. P. Arps and Adolph Langenfeld of New Holstein, Wisconsin, garnered much publicity for their Snow Birds and Snow Flyers. The White Snowmobile, developed in New Hampshire in 1923, did double duty as a sandmobile in the Egyptian desert. Carl Eliason of Sayner, Wisconsin, unveiled his Motor Toboggan in 1927.

Snowmobile, 1910

Arctic Cat, Inc., is headquartered in Thief River Falls, Minnesota. Polaris Industries, Inc., led by the Hetteen brothers, got its start in Roseau, Minnesota, in 1955. But it was the introduction of the lightweight Ski-Doo by J. Armand Bombardier of Quebec in 1958 that set off the snowmobile boom. With the advent of the Model T in

1908, many home inventors put engines on old sleds; Bombardier's first vehicle, tested in 1922, was a spindly Arctic sled with a motor mounted on top. It took a 1968 trip to the North Pole by four men riding heavy-duty versions of the Ski-Doo to put his snowmobiles on the map.

The pioneer who led the first snowmobile expedition to the pole was Ralph Plaisted, a Minnesota insurance agent and outdoor enthusiast. In 1966, with the permission of the Canadian government and the sponsorship of Bombardier Ski-Doo, he headed North with ten production models, an excellent two-way radio, extra fuel, and the finest lightweight provisions. Off they went in the spring of 1967, only to be turned back by a seven-day blizzard roughly 370 miles from their goal. But the snowmobiles performed admirably, so in 1968, equipped with even better Ski-Doos, Plaisted set out again accompanied by Jean Luc Bombardier (the founder's nephew), Walt Pederson, and Jerry Pitzel, all amateur Arctic explorers. After 43 days, 13 hours, and 52 minutes on rapidly melting ice, they reached the North Pole; their position was carefully verified by a U.S. Air Force plane using gyrocompasses. Unlike Peary and Cook, whose claims could never be checked, sixty years later Plaisted returned with a record backed by the U.S. military.

Purists insisted that traveling to the pole on a motor vehicle didn't really count. But Plaisted's record still stands. He was the first to get there via a surface route. Thanks to the reports of CBS newsman Charles Kuralt, who accompanied the first, unsuccessful attempt, and a *Life* magazine deal to publish the story, the public was all too ready to accept Ralph Plaisted, insurance agent, as a modern-day Peary with better equipment, including his trusty Ski-Doo.

form of cubes), and a finale in which Victor and the creature are crushed beneath the weight of a glacier collapsing the roof of the mountain cave in which they meet at last. Roger Corman's *Frankenstein Unbound* (1990), set in Los Angeles in the year 2031, flashes back to Mary, Percy, and Byron reciting dialogue full of portents and warnings. "Scientists," says the visitor from the future, "have made far greater monsters!" As for the North Pole, it has become the last refuge of atomic-age mankind, pulsing in the eerie light of a laser that fails to kill the monster.

The best of the recent adaptations, *Mary Shelley's Frankenstein* (1994), may not be as faithful a rendition of the book as the title would insist, but director and star Kenneth Branagh at least follows the structure of the original with some fidelity. The theme is the lust for knowledge and its dire consequences. It opens with scientist/explorer Robert Walton making for the North Pole in 1794 through a seascape based on the scariest details of a Caspar David Friedrich iceberg painting. Sailors scream in fright. Huskies yowl. And out of the blankness of the ice comes Frankenstein, the bloody pelts of his slaughtered dogs hanging above him like unholy banners on the altar of ego. Then, a flashback to Geneva in 1773—and the tale begins. Victor's noble intent, his growing arrogance, his fabulous pseudo-Victorian laboratory full of vats and chains, a meeting with the monster in an ice cave high in the Alps. The monster (Robert De Niro in a philosophic mood) rages on: What is my name? Who am I? Do I have a soul?

Denied a bride—Victor's revivified Elizabeth immolates herself rather than elope with the creature—the monster heads north for a final showdown with his "father." On a floating cake of ice, he stages a Shelley-like funeral for his creator, the berg breaks up, and a fragment, lit by the burning bier, floats off into the mist and disappears. The captain, yielding to the wishes of his terrified crew, turns for home. "Great God!" wrote Robert Falcon Scott in his journal on the day he realized he had been beaten in the race to the South Pole. "Great God! this is an awful place." At the end of the world, ambition finally dies.

One of the strangest reprises of the Frankenstein story came from the circle of Adolf Hitler and the Nazi Party in 1933. Throughout the years after World War I, German reactionaries had comforted themselves in defeat with a mythic Valhalla called *Thule*, found at the farthest reaches of the North. A kind of Eden for the master race, it was the cold, unspoiled homeland of the Aryan *übermensch*. The popular version of Thule was retailed in a series of cult films directed by Arnold Fanck in the 1920s—alpine fantasies full of glaciers, avalanches, and ice and featuring Leni Riefenstahl, Hitler's future cinematographer and rumored paramour, as the plucky heroine.

A "creative and visionary" Japanese gentleman, Masaru Emoto, claims that he can change the **STRUCTURE OF ICE CRYSTALS** by playing mood music as they form. In public experiments, he achieved dramatic results by playing a tune, typing a name onto a slip of paper, and taping it to a bottle of water overnight. When the contents were frozen, the water marked "Adolf Hitler" produced a dark, ominous shape. "Mother Teresa" ice was luminous and lacy.

The last and oddest of these Thulian epics was *S.O.S. Iceberg*, released in the United States by Universal Pictures with a fulsome dedication by the producer thanking the film crew for spending a year in Greenland, above the Arctic Circle, where "the slightest misstep meant death," and the Danish explorer Knud Rasmussen, under whose "protection" the project had been undertaken. Except for brief dramatic interludes, the picture is a romanticized documentary, a kind of hymn to ice, with the camera gliding among the fantastic shapes of immense coastal icebergs, lingering over those which seem to take on the Art Deco lines of the podium at a Nazi rally in Nuremberg. The slender storyline concerns a scientist trapped on a shrinking iceberg in the far North. He is rescued, after much ado, by his brave aviatrix bride (Leni, of course) with friends in high places and a brave Teutonic companion who swims for miles between the icebergs to reach an Eskimo village.

Filmed in crisp black and white, the nature scenes are still exhilarating to watch. The dramatic sequences are clumsy and too obviously staged inside giant igloos built by set decorators. But there is a Frankenstein monster in the form of a hirsute, squinty-eyed, overstuffed patron who insists on coming with the expedition. He complains, lags behind, knifes at least one explorer, pushes another into the drink, toys with the notion of cannibalism, and mugs the camera shamelessly. At last, just before the joyous rescue scene, he repents for no apparent reason and casts himself into the sea. And everybody else goes home, where they belong. Leni Riefenstahl's book about the making of the movie was titled *Kampf in Schnee und Eis*, her personal reprise of Hitler's *Mein Kampf*.

> Superman's **FORTRESS OF SOLITUDE** is a polar retreat made of pure, crystalline ice.

Hitler, so some of his rabid followers believed, escaped to Thule in an airplane in 1945 and lived there in a secret bunker, not far from the North Pole, that conferred immortality on those who called it home. The real Thule, in the northernmost corner of Greenland, was a tiny trading post named by Rasmussen in 1910. It is now the site of a "secret" American airbase left over from the Cold War era of A-bombs and missile silos. Scientists have indeed made monsters, as Mary Shelley predicted. But so have romantic dreams of human perfection.

4

ICE MADE, ICE FOUND, ICE SOLD

"I've been looking into refrigeration"

—

John Steinbeck, *East of Eden* (1952)

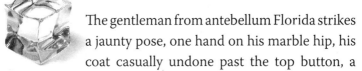The gentleman from antebellum Florida strikes a jaunty pose, one hand on his marble hip, his coat casually undone past the top button, a hint of a half smile upon his face. There he stands in the U.S. Capitol's National Statuary Hall between Frances Willard of Illinois and Robert Livingston of New York. Willard, a determined woman in a severe gown, was a prohibition advocate and president of the Woman's Christian Temperance Union. Livingston, a member of the Continental Congress, is semiregal in his bronze drapery; the man who administered the oath of office to George Washington and negotiated the purchase of Louisiana for Jefferson, he was a friend of inventor Robert Fulton. Fulton, in fact, named his

steamboat, the *Clermont,* after Livingston's sprawling estate. (Fulton, clutching a model of his *Clermont,* is honored in the same gallery—as a native son of Pennsylvania.)

The trio—Gorrie, Willard, Livingston—meets in odd proximity in the half-round gallery of great Americans adjacent to the House of Representatives. By provision of an act of Congress in 1864, the effigies were intended to be representative of the best the nation had to offer, no more than two from each state (each of which paid for the sculpture and chose the artists). The honorees were described as "deceased persons . . . illustrious for their historic renown."

John Gorrie, MD, duly selected by the State of Florida, was modeled in 1914 by local artist Charles Adrian Pillars, using the single surviving, anonymous oil portrait as his model. Today, when the Apalachicola community wishes to picture their homegrown hero in the tiny museum on Sixth Street dedicated to his accomplishments, a photo of the Statuary Hall Gorrie (1802–55) is generally used.

There are several tenuous connections between John Gorrie and his U.S. Capitol neighbors, however. On Bastille Day 1848, the French consul in residence in Apalachicola was determined to observe his own national holiday with a grand banquet at the Mansion House, the

John Gorrie, National Statuary Hall

seaport's best hotel. Just before July 14, during the hottest part of the summer (when the ice boats from New England's lakes had failed to arrive), he startled the brokers, merchants, and customs agents invited to the gala by declaring that his wines would be served cold. As the company prepared to toast Lafayette in tepid libations, the doors to the dining room were thrown open. In marched a phalanx of waiters bearing silver trays heaped high with blocks of ice. The champagne flowed—and it was cold, thanks to the man who made the machine that made the ice. "Let us drink to . . . Dr. Gorrie!" Gorrie was the inventor of a wonderful device that did nothing to encourage temperance or abstinence.

Unlike Livingston's associate Robert Fulton, Gorrie did not enjoy great success as an inventor. After the banquet, he had expensive models of his ice machine made. He roamed from Cincinnati to New Orleans to Charleston to Richmond seeking a backer to finance further operations. He gave demonstrations in hot-weather cities. And on May 6, 1851, he was issued U.S. patent number 8080 on his mechanism. Slogging his way through the slush-coated streets of New York in the winter of 1852, he hawked a fifteen-page pamphlet describing the process. Interest in *Dr. Gorrie's Apparatus for the Artificial Production of Ice in Tropical Climates* did not materialize, however. New Yorkers were caught up in the "science" of phrenology and the growing prospects of war with the South. The good doctor later claimed his failure was caused by the mockery of a hostile New York press whose editorials called the invention "a joke." "Some crank down in Apalachicola, Florida . . . claims he can make ice as good as God Almighty!" Gorrie smelled a plot, perpetrated by Frederic Tudor, the Boston "Ice King" who dominated the harvest and shipment of natural ice between the 1820s and the Civil War. Among Tudor's customers were the South's coastal cities, where Gorrie's machine—if successful—could have killed the business.

Thus, in life John Gorrie, MD and inventor, was not so lighthearted as the white marble statue's pose would suggest. A physician, public servant, and booster who tied his fortunes to the fate of Apalachicola—once a thriving Gulf Coast cotton market—he wore himself out tending to victims of the tropical diseases that ravaged the territory. Although Gorrie never quite made the connection between mosquitoes and Florida's annual fevers, he did come to believe that heat and the miasmas that arose from the "morborific" swamps in steamy summer weather were the culprits. If he could find a way to lower the temperature and purify the air, perhaps he could save his dying patients.

The answer was ice, in great quantities. And the immediate problem was that ice came to Florida on a hit-or-miss basis. Ships sank. Schedules changed. Up in the northeast, a warm winter meant a hotter July and August for the Ice King's Dixieland customers. One year in the early 1840s, Dr. Gorrie had the foresight to buy a wagonload of imported ice when it could be had, and he buried it in his sandy backyard entombed in sawdust. That summer, the price of ice rose to $1.50 a pound, if it could be purchased at all. Gorrie dug up his hoard, suspended basketfuls of ice from the ceiling of a sickroom, and connected the baskets to the chimney flue to maintain proper ventilation. The patient survived. All the good doctor needed now was a reliable supply of cheap ice.

He proposed to make it himself. Beginning in the 1770s, European scientists had tinkered with ways to make ice without cold temperatures. There is little doubt that Dr. Gorrie had read the pertinent literature on the subject. Struck by the theories of a Scottish physician, he began work on a practical ice machine—an evaporative process using a pump that reduced the atmospheric pressure in a vessel of water enough to produce ice. His device cooled fevers. It also chilled champagne.

The Gorrie machine depended on a fundamental law of physics. Namely, when a liquid is rapidly vaporized by

One-ton ice machine, 1922

compression, the expansion draws its energy from the air immediately around it. And the air becomes cooler as it loses energy. Using an arrangement of pumps and tubes, Gorrie compressed a gas, cooling it in a system of radiating coils and then expanding it again to lower the temperature still further. The gas-filled tubes then froze any water exposed to them. Voilà: artificial ice! Given that his machine cooled the air within it, there is some question as to whether the elegant mechanism now on exhibit in the Apalachicola Museum makes John Gorrie the "Father of Artificial Ice" or the "Father of Air Conditioning." As time passed without much profit from his work in either area, Gorrie himself concentrated on the benefits of refrigeration to mankind. "The cheap and abundant production of artificial cold," he insisted, "would enable many industrial arts to be carried on advantageously in warm climates, or continuously in temperate regions." In the end, however, he convinced nobody. Gorrie is probably best remembered as a seer, a utopian—and a noble failure. When he died in obscurity in 1855, the neighbors believed he may have taken his own life.

> **DRY ICE** is carbon dioxide gas compressed into a solid form. Colder than ice made from water, it is also denser and heavier. The name was trademarked in 1925 by an American firm. It is used for cryogenics, for shipping perishable goods, and for making artificial fog as the solid turns back into gas.

But Gorrie's quest to conquer disease led him into ever more basic inquiries. What is life? he asked. In the 1853–54 issue of a medical journal published in New Orleans, he posited that electricity was the secret to human vitality, attributing arterial blood pressure to electrical tension and magnetism. He believed to the end that he had discovered a basic principle of physiology that would revolutionize the study of circulation. Neither phrenology nor the dulcet arias of Jenny Lind moved him. Yet, like Victor Frankenstein and Mary Shelley, Gorrie had hit unerringly upon one of the popular scientific watchwords of his day: electricity—magical somehow, dangerous, the key to Earth's every mystery, including the secrets of the wandering poles at the planet's icy extremes. Electricity was preeminently the American science, the power of the world to come, founded by no less a personage than Benjamin Franklin, whose statue by Hiram Powers was installed in the Senate wing of the Capitol in 1862.

> NASA plans to crash a space probe into the South Pole of the moon sometime in 2009. The aim is to find LUNAR ICE, from which oxygen or rocket fuel could be made if the moon were to serve as an orbiting space station.

In 1854, as the first pages of John Gorrie's thesis on electricity and the blood were being distributed in New Orleans, Henry David Thoreau's *Walden* was published in Boston. On the Fourth of July 1841, Thoreau had moved into a cabin built with his own two hands on Ralph Waldo Emerson's woodlot at Walden Pond in Massachusetts. He was not, as popular mythology holds, a recluse. Thoreau walked into nearby Concord often, socialized with the Emersons, and felt the noisy energy of the modern world in the form of the Boston and Fitchburg Railroad, which skirted the pond in 1844. And he kept a journal of meticulous observations of nature that formed the basis for *Walden.* Emerson and the

American romantics of the transcendental school tended to see nature and the self as one. Thoreau did not. One of the reasons *Walden* is still widely read is for the pleasure of observing a lively, attentive intellect coming to grips with what he sees in the pond, the railroad cut, the changing of the seasons. His is a scientific vision unclouded, for the most part, by theory or utility. There is no money to be made, no disease to be cured—unless the ailment is human heedlessness.

The most engaging chapter of *Walden* is titled "The Pond in Winter." It opens with Thoreau awakening from a dream in which the ultimate questions—the whys and whats of human life—have been asked and left unanswered. But Nature, smiling in through his windows, puts no such queries. Life *is*—in the pines and the pond and the daylight. First the author chops a hole in the ice to fill his bucket. Then he turns his thoughts to the local fishermen trolling for pickerel through narrow slits in the ice, his survey of the pond's depth in 1846, and the arrival of the "ice-men" in the winter of 1846–47. The bosses had rejected some of the ice cakes sent to shore because they were not uniform in thickness with the others. Thoreau cites these findings as evidence for the existence of a hidden inlet to the pond. Before the incursion of industry, however, it was only the Concord landlord who had come with his ax to store up icy treasure—"solidified azure"—against the thirst of July.

The icemen of 1846–47 were Tudor's men, of course, a hundred Cambridge Irishmen, working the surface of Walden Pond for sixteen days like farmers in a field in the polar regions, "like a flock of arctic snow-birds." Thoreau describes the factory on the ice in full operation: the scoring, the sawing, the sledding to shore, the grappling, the stacking, the noon whistle, the horses eating their oats out of cakes of ice hollowed like buckets. Ironically, that ten-ton harvest (to which Thoreau had raised objections at the time) never got to market. It sat there in a pile covered with hay and was still not quite melted in September 1848. "Thus the pond recovered the greater part" of what business had taken away.

> An important ritual among ice fishermen is placing a bet on the date of the spring "ICE-OUT." This is the moment when a certain agreed-upon percentage of the ice on a given body of water has melted. Because ice melts from below, "ice-out" usually catches some sportsmen un-awares: pickups, snowmobiles, fish houses, and their owners sink to the bottom, creating a cottage industry in hauling lost gear out of lakes from New England to the Rockies. For those determined to win the jackpot, re-cords of past "ice-outs" are available to be studied over several beers with an attention usually reserved for base-ball statistics.

The last paragraph of his meditation on the ice is the most surprising. Thoreau suddenly realizes "that the swel-tering inhabitants of Charleston and New Orleans, of Ma-dras and Bombay and Calcutta, drink at my well." And that in a not-too-distant day, if things went according to plan, "pure Walden water" would be "mingled with the sacred water of the Ganges." It is a potent image, a powerful vi-sion of conductivity, of magnetism, of a current—albeit not an electric one—pulsing through the oceans to join Massa-chusetts with India. And in 1854 when *Walden* was issued, Frederic Tudor's firm was already sending ice to India on a regular basis; the ship *Arabella*, which made the trip to

Calcutta in 1854–55 (it took an average of 102.5 days) lost 76 percent of its original load to the heat but still managed to turn a profit.

The first cargo of two hundred tons of Tudor ice, cut from Fresh Pond and from the Kennebec River in Maine and packed in sawdust from Maine's timber mills, had arrived in Calcutta in 1833. The ice caused a sensation there. Some Indians responded with alarm when they touched one of these "crystal blocks of Yankee coldness," believing they had been burned. Others wondered if it grew on trees or bushes in America. The only ice ever seen previously in Calcutta was an "ooze" created by skimming thin sheets of surface ice from water poured into unglazed pots and left overnight in underground pits. The Tudor ice was

Cutting ice on the Kennebec, ca. 1895

such an improvement that local residents built an insulated icehouse exclusively for the imports. Before his global successes, however, Tudor had been ridiculed, jailed for debt, and nearly ruined because the idea of shipping ice around the globe seemed so ludicrous. In practice it was a hit-or-miss proposition at first. "No JOKE" read the headline in a Boston newspaper, announcing the departure of Tudor's first long-distance load in 1806.

> **ICE ROADS** made life easier for lumberjacks who felled trees in the northern forests during the winter months in anticipation of the spring thaw, when logs could be floated downriver to market. To move the timber from lumber camp to river, special crews constructed and maintained ice roads. The slippery surfaces allowed huge loads to be pulled readily by horse teams. First, a route was plotted, cleared, and packed with snow. Then came a water wagon or sprinkler to ice the surface. Next a "blue devil" gouged out ruts to fit the sleds' runners. In the 1890s, horses were gradually phased out by adapted steam engines. The most famous of these was the Lombard Steam Log Hauler, developed in Maine and patented in 1901. With log-fired engines and an arrangement of components dictated by the task at hand, haulers are ungainly looking machines. In that respect, they resemble the Lunar Landing Module used by American astronauts Armstrong and Aldrin in 1969. The module, like the log hauler, was designed from within—for function, not form.

Sailors refused to work on ice ships for fear that meltage would sink the vessels. Colonial governors often doomed the cargo by dragging out the customs process until there was no ice left to unload. Frederic Tudor and his brothers

met with disaster after disaster with ventures in Martin-
ique, Cuba, and other tropical ports. Only in the 1830s and
'40s, when Thoreau witnessed the Tudor ice harvest on
Walden Pond, did the business stabilize. Thanks to his own
efforts, Tudor's ice had become a highly desirable commod-
ity rather than a freakish novelty. In India, the iced gin and
tonic cooled spectators at polo matches. In the Caribbean,
coffeehouses served ice cream for the first time. In Apalachicola, Savannah, and New Orleans, the sudden arrival of
a Boston ice vessel was an occasion for celebrating.

Thanks to the efforts of Tudor's foreman, Nathaniel
Wyeth—grandsire of the painter-Wyeths—efficiencies in
harvesting increased profits, too. In January and February,
teams of horses dragged special machinery over the ice surface to remove snow and score regular blocks. Horsepower
lifted the blocks from the shoreline and moved them to the
nearest rail line. Horses helped to build slick ice roads over
which to slide blocks downhill to waiting wagons. Special
gangs with "shine sleighs" followed the horses, clearing away
the urine and pouring formaldehyde on the spots. With its
advanced "factory" system and vertical integration of cull-
ing, storing, shipping, and sales, the ice business was one
of the first modern industries. The ice trade also stimulated
other commercial activity. New England fisheries expanded
thanks to the practice of icing down the catch. Baldwin
apples went to England and her colonies packed in barrels
wedged among "ice-bergs" in the hold.

England was the major client for a product known
around the world as "Wenham Lake Ice," cut from a small-
ish lake in Massachusetts and prized for its purity, clarity,
and resistance to melting. Scientists, including the British

geologist Sir Charles Lyell, speculated on the reasons for its superiority, concluding that a lack of natural salts and debris and the area's sustained cold temperatures made for a peerless product. Certainly the American import was an improvement over English ice, a mushy mess often scraped up from roadside ditches and unfit for contact with edibles. Wenham Lake Ice, on the contrary, was advertised as suitable for table use. Like Tudor, the firms that pioneered the shipment of the Wenham product initially faced opposition; m'lords, on their first exposure to Wenham Lake Ice, insisted on adding hot water to their drinks. But by the 1840s, according to contemporary comments in the English press, "no banquet of any magnitude" was complete without it. Londoners gathered outside the company's office on the Strand, gazing on the block of Wenham ice always in

Hauling ice, 1870

the window. Or went inside to touch it, assuring themselves it was not a slab of glass. Some observers claimed it possessed such clarity that a newspaper might be read with ease through a two-foot block. Between 1844 and the mid-50s, "Wenham" and "ice" were synonymous terms. Visitors to the United States asked to be taken to Wenham Lake, imagining a body of water equal in size to Lake Superior.

One of the big news stories out of Iraq in the summer of 2007, as temperatures all over the United States soared into the torrid zone, was the shortage of **FACTORY-MADE ICE** in Baghdad. Without controls imposed by the Saddam regime, prices soared. Home refrigeration has been curtailed by power shortages. Factory-made ice is often impure—contaminated by chemicals and disease, especially in poorer neighborhoods. And going out to buy ice was extremely hazardous.

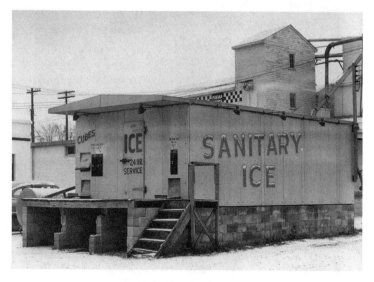

"Sanitary" ice dispenser, 1956

Airtight wooden boxes with interior shelves known as "Wenham Refrigerators" went on sale in London in 1845. Customers were warned to accept no substitutes; the genuine article was marked inside the lid with a metal plate bearing the company's coat of arms. The public at large was cautioned to be sure the ice they purchased was the real deal, too. The daily Court Circular, a listing of royal engagements, announced that Queen Victoria and her Prince Consort had tested the ice and found it a marvel of nature. By the end of the decade, a luxury item for Mayfair bluebloods was on its way to being a necessity for everybody else.

At midcentury, several practical means of producing ice in quantity through variations on the vapor compression method were already on the horizon. The long-distance ice shippers, to be sure, tried hard to discredit such devices: Dr. Gorrie may well have been correct in his belief that the Ice Kings of New England had done in his invention. But long before the shippers and the inventors battled for supremacy, people had found and stored ice for future use. Like making maple syrup from sap, ice cutting with the farmer's ax was a rural tradition, a cottage industry celebrated by Currier and Ives lithographs and fondly remembered by Americans who had left the farm behind. A Long Island lady's memoir of "the good old days" of her childhood paints a picture of her father using an ice saw on their pond and stacking the cakes in an icehouse near the kitchen door. That structure consisted of a deep pit roofed over and equipped with a door. Other such houses were built above ground with provision for drainage and double walls stuffed with protective grasses; roofs were often painted white to deflect sunlight.

Iceboxes

As late as the 1940s and early '50s, electrical refrigeration was still a luxury in many homes. Wartime rationing had all but stopped production of new appliances, and industry was slow to regain its consumer markets. The time-honored alternative to the "Frigidaire" was **THE ICEBOX,** a wooden cabinet lined with zinc or slate and insulated with charcoal. Under the bottom of the box, which was often adorned with fancy handles and curlicue name-plates, was a tray to catch the water that melted from the cakes of ice that kept the interior cool. The tray was impossible to empty without inundating the kitchen floor. Most kitchens were mopped daily with ice meltwater.

The ice came on a wagon—later a truck—in fifty- or twenty-five-pound blocks. Brightly colored cards with quantities printed in large letters on each edge were positioned in a front window as a signal to the iceman. A "50" on top meant that he should extract that quantity from the wagon, hoist it effortlessly up to his shoulder with a pair of lethal-looking ice tongs, and lug his burden up the stairs,

Ice delivery, 1930

around the path, through the door, into the icebox. No sign, no ice today.

> Walter Freeman, an eccentric doctor who was eventually elected president of the American Board of Psychiatry and Neurology, became a celebrity in the late 1940s and '50s for his cavalier use of the **ICE PICK LOBOTOMY**. He and his followers claimed to cure mental illness by taking a common tool used to chip ice off large commercial blocks, inserting it into the eye socket of a patient under local anesthetic, and rotating it vigorously to sever nerves at the base of the frontal lobe. Freeman liked to work in front of an audience. He even performed his surgery on TV shows. Lobotomies were used most often on women (including actress Frances Farmer) to control social behavior. Freeman persisted in lobotomizing the unruly and deviant until 1967, when he killed a female patient and was finally discredited.

Some houses had what were called "milk boxes" built into the kitchen wall. One locked door opened on the back porch. The other opened on the kitchen. In a pinch, the iceman could leave his burden in that box. Most homes had their own tongs for moving the ice. And all of them had ice picks, a square wooden handle with a sharp nail protruding from one end. Ice picks looked lethal and made for impromptu weapons in bars. At home, the wounded were more often than not children sneaking some ice chips on a hot day and skewering a hand in the process. Ice picks often came as premiums from the ice company but were also used to advertise soft drinks and ice cream brands.

Children flocked to bedevil the iceman for a stray chunk or asked to feed a carrot to his horse. He was a local hero, tough and strong. He was a neighborhood fixture like the postman, the milkman, the knife sharpener, the ragman, and the vegetable man, all nostalgic symbols today of urban life before freeways, supermarkets, two-car families, and big-box retailing. Old iceboxes have entered the living room and the den as prized possessions used to store DVDs—which won't melt on the wall-to-wall carpet.

Ice man, 1935

In Regency and Victorian England, the icehouse was a common feature of great estates in the form of garden "follies" or miniature Palladian villas. Commercial operations in Brighton, a center for the British trade, used pits or wells covered with brick domes as well as more conventional brick buildings with vaulted chambers and lead ductwork. American examples on the aristocratic model include an icehouse at Mount Vernon and another located in the north wing of Jefferson's Monticello. The latter held sixty-two wagonloads cut on the Rivanna River. The ice was used to preserve meat and butter and to chill the ice cream machine that had become a staple of elegant entertaining in Virginia. By the end of the antebellum period, however, ice had moved from the age of farmsteads and follies into a new industrial era.

> Playwright Eugene O' Neill took the title for *THE ICEMAN COMETH* (1946) from a popular joke in circulation at the time. The husband calls upstairs to his wife, "Has the Iceman come yet?" "No," she replies, "but he's breathing hard." Everybody got it! By this juncture, the Iceman had taken on the comedic status of the farmer's daughter in all-male barbershops and smoking cars.

In 1857, a shipment of natural ice from Norway (where a lake was hastily renamed Wenham) finally broke the American monopoly in Britain. In 1857, too, although the meat arrived "burned" by proximity to the coolant, an ordinary boxcar packed with dressed beef and ice successfully traveled from the Chicago stockyards to New York City. But 1857 is also the year in which the first insulated, ice-cooled refrigerator cars—the first "reefers"—took to the American rails on a regular basis. In 1842, the *American Railroad Journal* enthused over a new kind of freight car—a "summer-winter car"—used to transport perishable foodstuffs on the Western Line in Massachusetts. In hot weather, a cavity between the car's inner and outer walls could be filled with ice. In the winter, powdered charcoal would keep the cargo from freezing.

Although this visionary notion did not catch hold, lo-calized experiments continued and gained momentum after the Civil War, especially in the brewing industry. Americans preferred lager. That type of beer could be made only in the winter, however, until reefers full of chilled malt and hops extended the season indefinitely. The finished product, in kegs and barrels, was then dispatched using the same refrigerated freight cars, which often featured colorful trademarks emblazoned on the sides. Most of the ice used by both brewers and railroads in the 1870s was commercially made; the rapid growth in population, especially in the northern states, had already polluted the usual natural sources of harvested ice. And demand grew exponentially as the width of a continent often separated producers from consumers.

The most famous incident in the history of ice-cooled transportation occurred in the pivotal year of 1877, when Gustavus Swift of Chicago sent sides of beef to Boston in a reefer designed to retard both spoilage and damage from the ice. The burgeoning cities of the East were no longer able to supply meat from nearby sources; thus cattle ranching in the West became a booming concern. Beef shipped on the hoof from cowboy railheads like Dodge City and Abilene often arrived at the slaughterhouse in deplorable condition. In addition, Swift and other packers resented paying exorbitant freight rates on inedible parts of the livestock, which, they estimated, amounted to 60 percent of the total weight. The answer was doing the slaughtering, trimming, and processing in Chicago and sending only dressed sides of beef by train to butcher shops farther east.

After Swift and his competitors perfected the reefer, the Chicago Beef Trust soon displaced the Ice Kings by setting up an industry with the most highly coordinated production and distribution network of its time, reaching from the isolated ranches of Texas to the teeming streets of New York, London, and Bombay. They built their own ice plants and cold-storage warehouses. Their sheer volume of activity meant that Chicago could now dictate the price and the points of origin of vast quantities of ice. Chicago, in the words of the poet Carl Sandburg (1916), had become "Hog Butcher for the World" and "Freight Handler to the Nation." Chicago was also poised to become the Ice Capital of the industrial universe. The days of work gangs and horses swarming over the frozen surface of Walden Pond were over.

Among other things, ice was a marker for modernity, a sign of a fast-moving era in which luxuries became middle-class necessities and nature was challenged by technology. One of the charges brought against the rural South in the

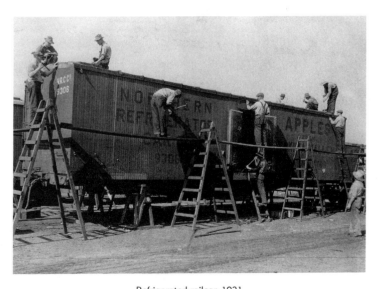

Refrigerated railcar, 1931

quarter century following the War Between the States was backwardness—Dixie was lackadaisical on account of the enervating climate. On the other hand, the tang of the air in cooler, northern climes made for *real* men, full of energy and drive. It could be argued that the quasi-suicidal expeditions to the polar regions in the late nineteenth and early twentieth centuries—those of Peary, Shackleton, Scott, and the rest of their intrepid band—were motivated by the sense of superiority ice conferred. Ice, or the confrontation between men and ice, bestowed a special grace of enterprise and vision throughout the Anglo-Saxon world.

Born in the sleepy, agricultural Salinas Valley of California in 1902, novelist John Steinbeck explored this ideology in *East of Eden* (1952), a retrospective saga based on his own family's dalliance with modernism and ice, circa 1915. Part 4, chapter 37 opens with the clan's father, Adam Trask, shaken awake by the growing century. He joins the Masons, subscribes to *National Geographic* and *Scientific American,* peers into the interior of his newfangled icebox, and buys a textbook on how refrigeration works. Then, a flash of inspiration hits in the form of an article about a mastodon discovered frozen in the Siberian ice field "for thousands of years. And the meat's still good." Adam haunts the local ice plant, examines the ventilated cars in which the railroads rush fresh fruit to market, and solicits backers for a plan to send Salinas lettuce to New York in cars cooled with ice. Skeptics brush him off. People don't want fresh produce in the wintertime, they say. If the cars get stuck on a siding somewhere, he'll lose the crop. "Let refrigeration alone."

Trask persists. The Chamber of Commerce stages a big departure ceremony: "Businessmen spoke of him as farseeing, forward-looking, progress-minded." The train departs pulling six carloads of lettuce packed in ice. Alas, the lettuce is held up for two days by a snowslide in the Sierras and arrives in Chicago during a heat wave. There the reefers sit, misdirected for another five days. When the train reaches New York, all that remain are "six carloads of horrible slop." Expenses for ice, freight, and cleaning out the debris almost bankrupt the Trask family and serve as the plot device that exposes ugly secrets from the past. The novel limps forward into World War I propelled by the consequences of tending to the future.

Director Elia Kazan, a close friend of Steinbeck, was among the first to read the novel in galleys and immediately took the book to Jack Warner for conversion into widescreen CinemaScope. From the beginning, Kazan intended to pare the sprawling novel down to size. He took the last eighty pages of the book—part 4—as his script. Steinbeck's Cain and Abel theme remained, with a twitchy James Dean in his first film role playing Cain ("Cal"). Thanks to his erratic performance and Raymond Massey's colossal stiffness in the role of Adam, the pictures register more strongly in memory than the characters. And the visual power of the movie comes from a series of repeated images of trains, lettuce, machinery—and ice.

A brass band plays off-key. The train leaves for New York, emblazoned with bold signs reading "Salinas Valley Lettuce." Suddenly, the scene shifts to an auto dealership, where the mechanic describes the operation of the Model T in excruciating detail. "Mr. Trask has just revolutionized the entire vegetable market," says Adam's partner. "Wait 'til those cars get to New York!" Technology is bringing modern times to Salinas—or vice versa. Suddenly, the sheriff arrives: "Big snow slide. Closed the pass and stopped the cars. . . . Can see water running out of the cars." This is Hollywood, so there are many more than six reefers, all of them leaking water at a furious rate, with Adam suddenly on hand to brood over the ruined crop. The extended scene sticks in memory when the rest of the film has faded to black. "It's still a good idea," insists Adam. "Cold can preserve things. Someday, somebody'll prove it."

While it is doubtful that any of theatrical crowd attending the benefit world premiere of *East of Eden* at Broadway's Astor Theater one warm March evening in 1954 knew their names, Gorrie, Tudor, and even Swift had seemed more eccentric than Adam Trask to their own contemporaries. Mounted to raise money for the Actors Studio, the screening itself was filmed and broadcast on television. The inside announcer read off a list of high-society attendees, although it was too dark to make out any of the "name" guests. The outside emcee, on a raised podium above the sidewalk, managed to coax Milton Berle, Margaret Truman, Eva Marie Saint, and other notables into camera range. Marilyn Monroe, a volunteer usherette, was hustled in a side door, pursued by Joe DiMaggio and a pack of reporters and photographers. Kazan, Steinbeck, Warner, and Massey did face the lens, however, looking tense and expectant: it was almost time for the Academy Award ceremonies on the opposite coast and Kazan's *On the Waterfront* was in the running for the Oscar. Nobody had much to say about *East of Eden.* And nobody said a word about ice.

5

ICE CASTLES

"It was a miracle of rare device /
A sunny pleasure dome with caves of ice"

—

Samuel Taylor Coleridge, "Kubla Khan" (1797)

January 1883. Clear and cold in Montreal. Cold enough for *Harper's Weekly* to have a little fun at the expense of America's neighbor to the north. "Dancing in an ice house," the editors remarked, "may strike the dweller in temperate zones as a somewhat stiff and spiritless form of recreation," even when the participants were fortified against bone-chilling cold with blubber, furs, and hot toddies. But this was no ordinary house: this was a full-blown palace made of ice harvested on the St. Lawrence River.

Rumor had it that the architect had stabilized the 150-foot central tower with timber and roofed it over with cedar brush before adding the ice. To some jealous Americans, at any rate, the electrified castle in Dominion Square did not quite measure up to chronicles of the all-ice wonders of the first such palace built in St. Petersburg by Czarina Anna in the eighteenth century. Hers was much smaller. On the other hand, *everything* was made of pure ice, from the windowpanes to the cannons that heaved ice balls heavenward with a mighty bang. In that respect, Canadians might well envy the Russians, whose Neva River usually froze to a depth of three feet. The colder the climate, the better the ice.

A subsequent *Harper's* report, written a week later, when the Montreal Ice Carnival was in full swing, observed that many of the event's features would be novel to tourists from the States who usually came to Canada in the warmer summer months. The castle, the carnival's most conspicuous visual symbol, was unforgettable. What American architect had ever dared to build a giant structure out of ice? Yet equal attention was paid to winter sports that had not found widespread popularity elsewhere—tobogganing, skating, snowshoeing, curling—and the clubs that sponsored them, all the while dressed up in colorful blanket coats, caps, and moccasins. Dreamed up by civic-minded boosters to keep the tourists coming year round, the Ice Carnival was an attractive example of making virtue out of necessity. Special chartered trains carried the governors of adjacent U.S. states and crowds of socialites up from New York and Boston for the festivities. And others looked on from greater distances in undisguised envy.

For the next several years, the Montreal carnival boomed. Minor royalty came from across the Atlantic. Balls and battles alike took on a starchy British flavor. But publicists also resurrected stories of the "Frost Fayres" held on the frozen River Thames during the Little Ice Age of the seventeenth and eighteenth centuries; there a carnival atmosphere had prevailed with all manner of lewdness, drunkenness, and gluttony. During the greatest of all these revels, in the bitter winter of 1813–14, a live elephant was paraded down the river. Diarists recorded that fly-by-night merchants set up shop in booths on the ice. A printer published a book entitled *Frostiana* in one of these temporary shelters. If Montreal was a bit too staid to welcome the Lord of Misrule to Place d'Armes, it did—in 1887—build a maze of ice there based on the famous model of Hampton Court.

In 2006, two Canadian businessmen shipped two hundred tons of **ICE MADE FROM DEOXYGENATED WATER** to London for use in constructing an ice palace three hundred feet long and seventy feet tall on the Thames. A recreated version of the palace was intended to tour Berlin and Barcelona for brief periods during the summer. Promoters counted on the "wow factor" to attract paying customers with the promise of biting cold and ice of amazing clarity.

After the first Montreal carnival, A. C. Hutchinson, the city's leading architect, decided that wood trusses and boughs had ruined the palace's fairy-tale magic. In 1884, the renamed ice castle was larger, grander, and almost transparent. As a "castle," Hutchinson's stupendous new version of palatial grandeur in ice became the site for a mock nighttime battle between attackers and defenders, members of the various sporting clubs equipped with torches and fireworks and singing club songs at the top of their lungs along the crenellated fortifications. This time, comparisons to the long-ago Russian model were weighted in favor of Canada.

The affair turned a profit—it was a business venture from the first—and plans went forward for more and better castles. In 1885, one hundred thousand spectators turned out for the battle. Its icy centerpiece was said to be the best castle yet, with a complicated cruciform shape and a snarling ice lion just outside the entrance.

But in the summer of 1885 as designs for the 1886 building were being drawn up, disaster struck. A smallpox

Henri Octave Julien, *Storming of the Ice Palace*, Montreal, 1885

epidemic broke out in the city, followed by riots on the part of those who feared vaccination. Within weeks, two thousand were dead. The United States sealed the border. An item in the *New York Times* seems to imply that a Montreal carnival took place regardless, but Americans did not attend and the planned castle was spoiled by an unseasonable midwinter heat wave. Instead, St. Paul, Minnesota, stole Montreal's castle—and its architect, too. The theft was a little surprising. Since 1883, scribes in St. Paul had been congratulating the city for its sensible attitude toward winter. Montreal, they thought, was courting disaster by advertising its snow and ice. The State Board of Immigration had, for many years, taken the opposite tack, insisting that the Minnesota climate was salubrious at all seasons, great for invalids, and suitable for growing any crop (with the possible exception of the date palm). But outside forces conspired to fill the collective mind of St. Paulites with revised visions of ice—beautiful ice, sparkly, wonderful, and profitable.

One such force was the pressure of a long-standing rivalry with Minneapolis, where devious ideas for outdoing the Saintly City were always circulating. The second was the offhand remark of a New York newsman who told the world that St. Paul was "another Siberia, unfit for human habitation in winter." The last was the weather itself. For three winters in a row—from 1883 to 1885—temperatures never rose above the single digits. The cold was unprecedented. There was ice as far as the eye could see. Siberia seemed tropical by comparison. So the movers and shakers summoned Mr. Hutchinson from Montreal and prayed for a hard freeze. St. Paul might not be Siberia or St. Petersburg, but it was the next best thing.

Some legendary czarist ice palace was almost always cited when a structure built of ice was mentioned. Almost always, too, the story varied from journalist to journalist, from orator to orator. The model was Peter the Great's ice palace—and he and his court had really lived in it! Other, nameless czars were said to have sealed up their enemies in prisons of ice and left them there to perish in the cold. Ice castles were an old Russian folk tradition with origins lost in the mists of time—ice huts or booths erected for riotous winter carnivals or *maslanitza*. Someone named Anna was the inventor—a semi-fictional czarina whose oddities and eccentricities Ivan Lazhechnikov had described in a novel called *Ledyanoi Dom* or *The House of Glass*. All these stories were half true. There *do* seem to have been ice palaces on the banks of the Neva River in the 1720s, during Peter's reign. There may have been another in 1734—a snow fort perhaps. But *the* ice palace was that of Anna Ivanovna, Peter's niece, who built the so-called House of Glass on the river in the winter of 1739–40, one of the coldest Europe had ever known.

Strange things happened that winter. In the falling temperatures, birds tumbled dead from the sky in the Ukraine. Around St. Petersburg, the river had frozen to such a remarkable depth that Anna was prompted to turn human misery into public joy by causing a palace to be built and opened to all comers. Or she was persuaded to do so in honor of the tenth year of her rule, her birthday, and the end of a disastrous war with the Ottoman Empire. Or it was another of Anna Ivanovna's grotesque jokes. Shunted aside by Peter, married off to the ruler of a grim little duchy strategically placed between Prussia and Poland (her duke died of drink almost immediately after the marriage festivities), Anna came back to Russia and the throne unexpectedly in middle age, tall, fat, and surrounded by German plotters and sycophants. Her face would stop a clock; her huge ruddy cheeks looked like a pair of Westphalian hams. Her only real pleasures in life were shooting game and tormenting her court jesters.

> H. Rider Haggard's Edwardian potboiler *She* (1887) was made into a 1935 science fiction film starring Helen Gahagan. The novel was set in Africa in the land of Kor, ruled by a vicious but beautiful immortal called Ayesha (aka SWMBO, or "She Who Must Be Obeyed"), guardian of the Flame of Life. Hollywood moved the setting to **THE RUSSIAN ARCTIC AND AN ART DECO ICE PALACE**, in which stylized Busby Berkeley–style dance numbers take place around a cauldron of fire. The movie lost money. Some say that its failure drove its star into politics.

When Peter had married Anna off years before, the wedding feast was crowned with a giant pie. The crust was sliced open and out popped an assortment of dwarfs, fools, hunchbacks, members of exotic tribes plucked from the four corners of the kingdom, and discredited aristocrats demoted to the rank of unwilling comics. As ruler of all the Russians, Anna continued the practice of collecting odd people, a belated echo of the customs of the Italian Renaissance courts. The House of Glass was intended as the mock bridal bower for a couple selected from her human menagerie. The groom was an aged prince, reduced to sitting on a nest and cackling like a chicken for the empress's amusement. The bride, a Kalmuck serving woman called "Buzhenina" after the ruler's favorite dish (roast pork in spiced vinegar), was surpassingly ugly. And inside the ice palace was a nuptial chamber in which the bed and bed curtains, the mirror, the dressing table, a working clock, and even two pairs of little slippers were carved from ice. The pair was sealed up in the house in a kind of satire on marriage rituals but survived to tell the tale and to produce at least one set of twins. Lest the modern reader be tempted to condemn Anna's actions, it is well to remember that pretend weddings almost as peculiar as this one were still being celebrated in the civilized twentieth century. Children, men dressed in ladies' clothes, and animals dressed in human garb all walked down aisles scattered from Warsaw to Des Moines. Marriages consecrated in strange places—from midair (skydivers) to the bottom of the swimming pool (scuba divers)—were hardly unknown. Anna Ivanovna's story has been put in a special category, however, not only because of the unfortunates involved but also for her habitual brutality toward those who offended her. The clucking prince is one mild example. Peter Eropkin, designer of the House of Glass and devotee of its elegant Palladian style, was sentenced to be quartered and beheaded on dubious charges of treason shortly after his masterpiece melted away. Only at the last minute was his punishment reduced to a simple beheading. His alleged fellow conspirators were variously impaled alive or had tongues and limbs chopped off before their hideous executions. In eighteenth-century Russia, historians of the era blandly observe, the combination of barbaric cruelty, peasant humor, excesses of all kinds, and great art was not in the least unusual.

The art of the House of Glass as well as the details of its construction were set down in 1741 by Georg Wolfgang

Krafft, a German-born professor of physics at the Russian Academy of Sciences in St. Petersburg. His treatise was best known in the West (where Coleridge may have used it as the model for his "caves of ice" in "Kubla Khan") thanks to a contemporaneous French translation by Pierre Louis LeRoy. Krafft's *Description et Représentation Exacte de la Maison de Glace,* complete with descriptive engravings and an account of the ceremonial goings-on at the *maison,* was the major source for later embellishments upon the blood-soaked saga of Anna and her Palladian ice villa on the Neva River.

Russian ice palace interiors

That villa occupied a prime piece of real estate between the Admiralty and the Winter Palace. Yet for all the fuss and the thirty thousand rubles spent on the project, it was not very large—about thirty-three feet in height, eighty feet long, and divided internally into three chambers. According to Krafft, each block of ice was precisely measured and chosen for its absolute transparency. The cakes were fitted together with freezing water so smoothly that the whole building seemed to have been carved from a single shimmering iceberg. There were niches, statues, naked putti, trees fashioned from ice, ice chinaware, a working bathhouse made of ice logs, and an ice elephant that spewed fire from his trunk. The six ice cannons may have been of Professor Krafft's own invention. The only "real" objects in the compound were the playing cards frozen into the surface of a parlor table.

Georg Krafft was dazzled by the perfection of the House of Glass, whose walls seemed to have been fabricated from some rare bluish-green marble that glinted eerily in the moonlight. But he also mused on the transience of ice. Unlike precious stones, ice would soon vanish into nothing more than a lovely memory. And it did, with amazing rapidity. By March, the building was in ruins. By June, it was little more than a few bits of floating ice bobbing in the Neva. By year's end, the architect and the empress were both dead, too. Only the stories, the rumors, the lovely memories, and a few enigmatic snatches of poetry were left. William Cowper, an English poet a generation younger then Empress Anna, marveled at the legend of a palace built without the aid of quarry or forest but hewn from water, "thy marble of the glassy wave."

In 2003, in honor of the three-hundredth anniversary of the founding of St. Petersburg—his hometown—Russian

Federation president Vladimir Putin authorized a massive program of renewal and historic restoration there. One result was an almost-faithful reconstruction of Anna's House of Glass. The for-profit ice palace differed from the prototype in only two important respects: instead of captive jesters, the bedroom was occupied by an ice effigy of Anna frozen to her chair, and a copy of the city telephone directory was added to the frozen playing cards in deference to a major corporate sponsor. Russians shivered in long lines to peek inside; ten thousand tickets were sold at five dollars apiece. Recalling the original usage, backers planned to offer the new House of Glass to bridal pairs for four-hundred-dollar weddings (four thousand dollars if they insisted on staying the night). Capitalism had arrived in St. Petersburg over some few feeble objections to spending huge sums on a frivolity. A reborn artifact of Russian heritage and pride, Anna Ivanovna's ice fantasy continues to be rebuilt annually as a five-hundred-ton tourist attraction of amazing, ethereal beauty.

The evanescent fragility of ice castles, a kind of sadness that underpins the splendor, was one of the perverse attractions of their kind. F. Scott Fitzgerald's short story "The Ice Palace," first published in 1918, explores the mixed feelings of regret, nostalgia, strangeness, and attraction aroused by the gaudy too-muchness of the St. Paul ice works of the 1880s. When Fitzgerald actually composed his story in 1917 or '18, the winter carnival ice palace was being revived after a long hiatus. These newer versions were backgrounds for sports rather than three-dimensional dwellings of make-believe North Wind royalty who played out the mythological story of the annual battle between a persistent winter and summer's inevitable arrival.

A Minnesota folk-rock quartet calls itself **ICE PALACE**. Reviewers claim to hear a sad, wintry quality in their music. At first, members denied any meaning to the name: they were just looking for a phrase with no connections to anything—no cold songs and no ice songs. But their resolve crumbled. They now cite F. Scott Fitzgerald's short story of the same name as the origin of their moniker. "It's not big St. Paul pride or anything," says bassist Sarah Schneeberger. "I've never been to the winter carnival, although I do like the idea of an ice palace."

So Fitzgerald's text hearkens back to notable palaces of the 1880s and describes their features—interior rooms, a labyrinth, a "Canuck" architect—rather than the more perfunctory constructions of his own day. Although he also approvingly quotes the "caves of ice" passage from "Kubla Khan," his St. Paul ice palace is a fearsome, cold riddle. Sally Carrol Happer, a nineteen-year-old visitor from the Deep South, finds herself lost among her fiancé's chilly Minnesota friends and then really lost—abandoned—in the labyrinth's chambers beneath the carnival palace (there was an ice maze in the 1887 structure). Sally Carrol, unlike Fitzgerald's own Southern-born Zelda, flees back to the emotional warmth of home.

Air conditioning and central heating have done a lot to undermine the stark physical contrasts of "The Ice Palace": the Deep South of the twenty-first century is too cold in the summer and the legendarily Frozen North often too warm in the winter. What still rings true, however, is the fervor with which Minnesotans took to palace building—and continue to do so. The Rockies may offer a better lineup of winter sports. There are great year-round castles at Disneyland and the Magic Kingdom in Florida. But nothing defines

Minnesota better than its communal pride in creating lovely things under extreme conditions. In 1886, the first St. Paul ice palace was the largest such entity ever built, bigger by far than Anna's bridal bower or Montreal's North American exemplar. One hundred fifty thousand people doled out a quarter apiece to walk inside. Clubs for skaters and sledders and curlers sprang up overnight, each with its own gaudy hats and blanket coats. At the laying of the cornerstone, ice blocks arrived from towns and cities across the state and the nearby Dakota Territory.

Everybody wanted in on the act, from the "Canuck" architect to the crews that cut ice on the Mississippi to the committees that begged the architect to make it bigger and bigger still, despite a nasty thaw at the end of December. They contrived, all of them, to build a palace that was twice as big as anything Montrealers had ever dreamt of. More

St. Paul ice palace, 1886

than that, it was a thing of great glittering beauty, a symbol of hardship turned to wonderment and joy. It was a symbol, too, of America's simmering drive to become a global power; an exhibition of the Arctic "Greely relics" inside Fitzgerald's ice cave was one of the Minnesota festival's highlights. Science, art, local pride, and imperial ambition joined hands in a romp through the snowy streets of St. Paul. "The whole city," exclaimed *Harper's Weekly*, "has given itself up, heart and pocket and hand, to the spirit of the carnival."

The so-called relics—boots, gloves, a sled—were the remains of a scientific expedition led by Adolphus W. Greely, a signal officer sent out in 1881 with twenty-four companions in search of a missing polar expedition. Greely was also instructed to set up a study lab or station above the Arctic Circle at Lady Franklin Bay on Ellesmere Island. Then he and his men vanished onto the polar ice. Thanks to a tragicomic series of blunders, relief expeditions sent to find him in 1882 and 1883 succeeded only in missing their quarry at every opportunity. In the meantime, Greely joined the self-destructive international race for the "farthest North" and the glory of taking the honors from the British. When help finally came, only seven men remained alive, huddled in a deflated tent, fewer than forty-eight hours from their mortal end. No one recognized Greely and the others at first— until the hairy, emaciated, unwashed leader croaked out the news that he had "beaten the record," at 83°24′ N. "Here we are," he added, "dying like men." For his feat, Greely was made a brigadier general. Before setting out for the pole with Matthew Henson in 1909, Peary enviously noted the honors and the fat exhibition fees garnered by those who went before him. And 83°24′ N wasn't even the pole!

After Greely was rescued, he was accorded a gala welcome in his native Newburyport, Massachusetts. Triumphal arches were decorated with inspirational words—"Hard the Struggle, Great the Victory!"; "Hail to the Hero!"; "The Frozen Seas Give Back Our Son!" The latter text appeared on an Arctic arch made of simulated ice and topped off with a pair of sculpted polar bears. Commemorative poetry honored the dead and praised the living: "High had their zeal for science burned— / It lighted Greenland's domes. / Oh God! the dreadful months of pain, / The months of living death!" Newspapers speculated on the southward drift of the polar ice that bedeviled Greely's party, noting that American cities had grown so cold in the summer months that it was no longer necessary to flee to the beach during steamy Julys and Augusts. Was the temperature of the whole continent plummeting? Could the navy *please* park a fleet of battleships off Labrador to explode any icebergs apt to wander toward the U.S. coast?

> At the end of 1942, four U.S. Army airmen took off from Sacramento on a training run and never came back. In 2006, a hiking party on the Mount Mendel Glacier found a man preserved intact—except for his protruding head and right arm—in a four-hundred-pound block of ice. The remains proved to be those of an aviation cadet, one of the four missing for more than sixty years. Finding the body of an MIA in the United States partially **EMBEDDED IN A GLACIER** was an all-time first in American military history.

Once the joyful hoopla died down, however, some ugly rumors about the Greely expedition began to circulate. Corpses were exhumed and examined. Survivors were deposed. Evidence of cannibalism surfaced. Greely's hero status came into question. None of this adversely affected the packaged showings of the "relics," however. Until Peary publicly claimed the North Pole for his own on April 6, 1909, artifacts from Greely's mission were greeted with interest by patriotic Americans at fairs and festivals, regardless of the whispers—or because of them. The land of ice and snow was clearly a mysterious and dangerous place. With its spectacular ice palace, St. Paul's Winter Carnival reinforced the sense of mystery and wonderment attached to the North. But absent scurvy, cannibalism, and madness, it also tamed and domesticated the terrors of the ice caps. In the carnival's context, the quest for the farthest North

St. Paul ice arch, 1887

Leadville ice palace, 1896

was a bit of a game, like the annual snowshoe races around the palace.

Interest in the St. Paul Winter Carnival—especially the massive expense and effort involved in castle building—peaked in the late 1880s. Thereafter, the decision to build was made on a hit-or-miss basis, affected by the weather and the current financial climate. Some palaces melted into rubble. Some were planned but never started. In 1896, although St. Paul did put up a respectable palace, Leadville, Colorado, temporarily captured the spotlight with a giant Norman castle built as a way to prop up the sagging economy of the former mining town. To guarantee success, the town fathers hired C. E. Joy of St. Paul, the architect of several Minnesota ice palaces (and the person responsible for hiring Hutchinson away from Montreal in 1886). There are conflicting accounts of the success of Joy's Leadville ice palace. The city never built another one. The estimated costs soared out of sight. Visitors who trekked to Leadville on excursion trains spent next to nothing in town and left early. The weather refused to cooperate: photographs show battlements left incomplete or crumbling away in the unwelcome thaw. On the other hand, there were trout, steaks, and pickles frozen into the walls as ingenious ads for the palace restaurant, a series of permanent wooden buildings inside the enclosure that were meant to outlast the castle, and an impressive show of locally manufactured goods. But finally, after use as a barracks for militiamen called out to suppress an ugly miners' strike, everything was torn down and forgotten.

> Where's the **"ICEBOX OF THE NATION"**? For as long as anybody can remember, it's been International Falls, Minnesota. That's where corporate America always tested out its cold-weather products and filmed ads for ice-worthy pickup trucks. Indeed, the slogan had even been registered by the city fathers. But in 1996, say the elders of Fraser, Colorado, the nickname was canceled or allowed to lapse. Even though Garrison Keillor wrote a special song about International Falls and sang it to his audience of 4.3 million listeners in 2007—the aim was to induce much-needed doctors to relocate there—Fraser continues to press its claim. Keillor's fetching lyric? "In the dead of winter it can feel like outer space / But for the right kind of person it could be the perfect place."

The modern world has never been quite sure what to do with ice palaces. The material itself is hardly a wonderment anymore, and life, for the most part, takes place in artificial climates that blur the differences between hot and cold. In a sense, ice palaces are frivolous anachronisms, summoning up visions of a long-ago time when communities were formed around arcane rituals, a cadre of social and civic leadership standing at arm's length from the political process (or above it), and a taste for club membership. A good example of a throwback to the castle craze of the nineteenth century is the *Carnaval de Québec*, inaugurated in 1955 in Quebec City on the model of earlier festivities. Beginning in 1893, the old French city had built large, impressive ice fortresses opposite Parliament, along with such memorable adjuncts as a fifty-foot beer bottle made of ice, a replica of the Eiffel Tower (a "living arch" made of greenery), and a real Eskimo igloo at the center of an ice maze. Other memorable constructions of the decade included a ziggurat or Tower of Babel, a giant snowball, and a windmill made of colored ice. The intention clearly was to best Montreal, and the roll call of foreign guests on hand—including the John Jacob Astors—suggests that Quebec did so. But the expense took its toll on government coffers. The ice palace tradition revived in the 1950s was not a continuous one.

The reborn Quebec Carnival, less sports-oriented than its predecessors, is a raucous, pre-Lenten Mardi Gras presided over by Bonhomme, a seven-foot mascot or patron saint in the form of a jolly, rowdy snowman dressed in a French Canadian hat and sash. He is the Lord of Misrule, and his sites of revelry, his palaces, are built for dancing and parties and fun. In the early years, people judged to be too gloomy during the festivities could be locked up in an ice jail adjacent to the castle. Until 1993, the anniversary year of the first Quebec ice palace, many of the palaces and prisons were made of huge bricks of compacted snow: now ice is back in fashion. While the founder of the renewed winter carnival speaks of "making winter bearable," the event is big business, with corporate sponsors—the number-three enterprise in the province, so the organizers boast, and the mainstay of the region's tourist industry. Ice turns a handy profit.

> **FROZEN DEAD GUY DAYS**, celebrated each March in Nederland, Colorado, is an excuse for a weekend of fun and profit. A local man cryogenically frozen by his grandson as part of a scheme to fund a Life Extension Institute was found in a tin garden shed, abandoned by the family. After the tabloid press discovered the "dead guy," local promoters were quick to capitalize on his notoriety. In 2001, he was treated to a 101st birthday party: a slice of cake was deposited in his preservation capsule. The revels continue with an annual look-alike contest, pieces of his original shed for sale, and escorted champagne visitations to his new repository.

But the magic memory of ice palaces reaches far beyond the frigid Plains of Abraham, where the walled city of Quebec stands. The autocratic president-for-life of Turkmenistan, a former Soviet republic, is famous for a series of peculiar decrees issued in the 1990s, after the collapse of the Soviet Union. Saparmurat Niyazov changed the word for *bread* to his late mother's name. He made applicants for a driver's license pass a morality test and put golden statues of himself everywhere. In 2004, after a controversial meeting with Canadian Prime Minister Jean Crétien to discuss an oil deal, he decided to replace the traditional Seven Wonders of the World with a new group to be located exclusively in Turkmenistan. The first of them, which was scheduled to begin construction in August 2004, was to be the largest ice palace ever made. If completed—and there are no signs that it will be—his would have been the first ice palace built in a desert in the heat of summer.

With the centennial of the St. Paul Winter Carnival approaching in the 1980s, the city sprang into action to produce not simply a replica of the 1886 ice palace but something grander and more beautiful—a true wonder of the world. Planned as a one-time-only event, construction was financed through the sale of handsome ice block certificates suitable for framing. Craft and labor unions volunteered their skills, 750 members strong. Old tools for ice cutting (nine thousand blocks) were located in Colorado: it is tempting to believe that they were "relics" of the old Leadville debacle. A TV station donated the cost of liability insurance: ours, alas, is a more litigious time. A statewide contest was held for a design, and the winning entry centered on four slender Towers of the Winds, each representing a season of the year. The biggest, projected to rise 150 feet, was eventually scaled back to 128 feet by rising temperatures, but the castle still took official honors as the tallest ice building in history in

St. Paul ice palace, 1986

the *Guinness Book of World Records*. Because of the terms of the insurance policy, however, visitors were kept outside: the Centennial Ice Palace was an object of crystalline contemplation rather than a bar, a marriage bed, or a desperate plea to rescue St. Paul from penury.

Six years later, St. Paul did sponsor a second modern ice palace for practical reasons. Its twin city of Minneapolis hosted the Super Bowl in 1992; not to be outdone, St. Paul countered with a last major effort at tempting tourists to venture across the Mississippi. The new palace was not much to look at, the effect of transparency spoiled by pinnacles fashioned of brightly colored tenting. Again, there were no entrances. It was strictly a spectacle, demanding little of attendees except a small fee and a passive attitude. Yet the palace cost twice what had been estimated—almost $1.9 million. The debt was eventually written off, but the winter carnival to date has attempted no additional architectural feats.

Today's last bastions of ice building are found in Asia. Harbin, China, and Sapporo, Japan, both host annual contests with divisions for snow sculpture and architecture and with competitors drawn from an international circuit which also makes stops in St. Paul and Quebec City. But the trajectory of ice palace history has tended increasingly toward the profit sector. Ice architecture in the twenty-first century consists of two forms. One is the smattering of ice hotels in Canada and Northern Europe that cater to eccentric tastes in accommodations—or memories of Empress Anna's frigid bedchamber. The other is the faddish ice bar. Often sponsored by vodka distillers, the bottles, furniture, and decor are all made of ice. The twelve-thousand-pound

Ice Chamber Bar in the new Chambers Hotel in Minneapolis, opened in the winter of 2007, is the ice palace of the future—and pretty, fur-clad bartenders report getting lots of "sympathy tips" from customers chilled to the bone in the name of fashion. Internet firms that cater to the trade advertise their ability to deliver almost anything carved in ice: chandeliers, Art Deco ice bars, and corporate symbols for parties, including a six-foot Coke bottle and a moon rocket. The same items, of course, also come in simulated plastic ice. The going price for lifelike artificial ice cubes, with interior bubbles and fissures, is fifteen dollars a dozen. The same firm that makes the cubes can also supply blocks, icicles, and, if needed, teensy mini-icebergs.

Dubai in the United Arab Emirates, where the usual summer temperatures hover at 111°F, has welcomed "CHILLOUT," THE FIRST ICE LOUNGE in the Middle East. Tables and chairs, walls, dinner plates, glasses, curtains, the art on the wall—and a seven-foot chandelier over the bar—are all made of ice. The cover charge includes parka and glove rental. The ice was cut and carved in Canada.

6

ICEBERGS

"Detonations and falls were heard on all sides,
great overthrows of icebergs"

—

Captain Nathaniel Palmer, log of the *Hero*, November 17, 1820

Robert Falcon Scott, who perished in 1912 on his way back from an unsuccessful effort to be the first to reach the South Pole, was a strange, contradictory character. Antarctic exploration of the era may have demanded the odd combination of sentimentality, pigheadedness, and amateur science Scott exhibited in the posthumous version of his *Journals,* which appeared in 1914 with an introduction by J. M. Barrie, the celebrated author of *Peter Pan* (1904). The two were well acquainted. Scott's only child, born in 1909 shortly after the fatal expedition was announced, was called Peter after Barrie's hero. Commentators have remarked that "Con" Scott's description of the death of one of his companions was borrowed from Barrie's memorable scene in which Wendy Darling hopes that the sons of England will always die like gentlemen. Captain Oates, days before the rest of Scott's handpicked polar party succumbed to cold, hunger, and scurvy, simply left the tent and crawled off into a gale. "I am just going outside and may be some time," he said, very like an English gentleman leaving a drawing room—and never returned.

The same Scott who could fret endlessly over how to divide the rations could also, like many an Englishman before him, neglect the finer points of skiing, dogsledding, and the use of igloos because they were not the ways of proper Britons. But on one point—the appearance of icebergs—he indulged in fantastic descriptions of light and beauty that rival Barrie's Tinker Bell (an invisible sprite always represented on the stage by a darting spotlight). At first, as the good ship *Terra Nova* plunged south from New Zealand, icebergs were objects to be categorized and measured: were

Herbert Ponting, *Castle Berg*, 1911

the layers of blue ice visible between tiers of white a sign of the action of thawing and refreezing? But once in the thick of the ice pack, moving warily to avoid collisions, Scott left the classifying to his science officers while he began to admire the shapes and colors of the icebergs shining on a sea of dazzling blue. He rejoiced at the pink of the evening sky. The "bergs . . . to the north," he wrote, "had a pale greenish hue with deep purple shadows" as the heavens themselves shaded to saffron and then green. "No art can reproduce such colors as the deep blue of the iceberg."

Herbert Ponting, Scott's resident photographer, took pictures that have come to define the Heroic Age of polar derring-do. One shot in particular shows what expedition members dubbed the "Castle Berg," stranded temporarily on the ice shelf in McMurdo Sound. It was "the most wonderful iceberg ever reported in the polar regions," Ponting rhapsodized. The shape was pure romance, evocative of a medieval castle with a high turret at one end and lofty battlements on every side. The berg's immense height was demonstrated in Ponting's picture by a tiny sled team and driver in the foreground, plodding across the frozen sea. His best-known photo from Scott's final expedition was taken from the depths of a striated cave deep within an iceberg, looking out toward the *Terra Nova* and the gelid expanse of the Southern Ocean. "A veritable Aladdin's Cave of Beauty," Scott wrote, but the view is also unforgettable as an emblem of humankind's humility and bravery in the face of nature.

Photographers who spend time in Antarctica today are drawn to the icebergs' otherworldly forms: flat-topped tabular bergs, like fragments of Cubist paintings, rising to great heights; battered bergs, eroded by wind and time into castles or storm-tossed Art Deco trees or sci-fi rocket ships; and rounded, pillowed bergs, like homemade birthday cakes, formed when the whole mass of ice flips over in the water, exposing a sea-smoothed underside. During the brief austral summer, photographers come in tourist ships: although the Inuit peoples of the North are said to have twenty-three words for varieties of ice, seeing is believing. Interlopers come for longer stays during the winter months on grants from the National Science Foundation's Office of Polar Programs or as employees of the various national groups and businesses that staff a host of polar stations. They come to see ice in all its shapes and guises, a landscape that is as close to the terrain of Mars or the moon as any place on Earth.

> The experts disagree: do the indigenous peoples of the North have **TWO HUNDRED DISTINCT WORDS FOR ICE**—or seventy-six? Or only twenty-three?

On the worst days of his futile trek toward the pole, Scott looked out upon the landscape of snow and ice and wondered if anything could "be more terrible than this silent, wind-swept immensity." But viewed from the safety of land or the deck of a vigilant, steel-hulled excursion ship, icebergs are the essence of beauty, gliding past on their erratic journeys into nothingness like dreams, imaginings, mirages. Old sailors, wise in the ways of the cold, observed long ago that the polar air itself turns perceptions upside down: faraway mountains reflected in wafting ice crystals become will-o'-the-wisp castles dancing in the sky. This peculiar cold-weather mirage, called a *fata morgana*, was named after King Arthur's fairy sister, Morgan, who lived in a crystal palace under the sea and built wondrous sky castles

Bradford, Dunmore, and Critcherson, "This View Shows the Beautiful Forms in Varied Shapes which the Berg Assumed," *The Arctic Regions*, 1869

out of pure imagination. Icebergs are an enchantment, a siren song from the stars.

There is a long tradition of photographers inspired by the otherworldliness of Antarctica. Scott had Ponting. Ernest Shackleton and Douglas Mawson had the Australian Frank Hurley. Minnesota-based Stuart Klipper, whose immense panoramic shots of glaciers, ice fields, and bergs have been featured at the Museum of Modern Art, sees the South Pole region as "extraterrestrial . . . an edge . . . a place where, on earth you feel more [a] part of the firmament than perhaps anywhere else." His first trip to Antarctica came in 1987, aboard a sixty-one-foot yacht. As an NSF artist and an adventurer, he has returned repeatedly, toting his bulky Linhof Technorama, in search of ways to tell what it's like to be at the last place on earth, where there is no more.

His iceberg portraits—and they are portraits—have a presence that does not rely on evocative contrasts between

vast ice castles and miniscule human intruders. The icebergs
are themselves, alien and strange, stopped for a moment of
confrontation by the snap of a shutter. They are physical
entities seen in great detail, carrying with them the marks
of eons and yet, like the photographer who stalks them,
mortal. Klipper read the stories of Scott and the others as
a child. But he has seen that ice is more complicated than
the heroic tales would allow, despite the explorers' delight
in a vocabulary of technical words for its states and quirks
of surface. Ice, in some hard-to-define way, remains inde-
scribable and unknowable.

The Celtic rune for *ice* (Ee-saw) is a single, unadorned
vertical line. In divination rituals, it stands for stasis and
stagnation, cooling emotions, concentrated power, and danger. In *20,000 Leagues Under the Sea* (1870) by Jules Verne,

Stuart Klipper, *Ice Floe*, 2000

the father of modern science fiction, icebergs have a chapter all their own in which beauty, danger, immobility, and steely ambition compete for dominance. The *Nautilus,* a futuristic Victorian submarine commanded by the mysterious and dictatorial Captain Nemo, seizes two shipwrecked travelers and sets off into an ice field full of bergs. The story's narrator is dazzled by the array of colors presented by the icebergs, which remind him of precious gems—enormous amethysts piled up to create "Oriental towns with . . . mosques and minarets." But suddenly, an iceberg turns itself over and traps the submarine hundreds of feet below the ocean surface with the air supply running short. Prisoners of the iceberg, the unwilling passengers nonetheless admire the underside of its "dazzling mine of gems" until Captain Nemo works the vessel free and heads for the South Pole. On March 21, 1868, he becomes the first to reach the elusive goal, forty-three years before Roald Amundsen arrived there.

Icebergs are chunks that break off from ice shelves on the margins of land or from glaciers as they flow into the world's oceans. The process of disengagement is called "calving." Glaciers themselves are formed by the gradual compression of accumulating snowfalls over the course of thousands of years. Scientists believe that a snowfall in West Greenland in 1000 BC might eventually appear as an iceberg calved into Baffin Bay and the North Atlantic from the Jakobshaven or the Humboldt Glacier, circa 1993. Old ice is extremely hard and cold (-20 degrees); the salt has been squeezed out by the weight of successive snowfalls, leaving behind a pure bluish substance that floats with ease. Between ten and fifteen thousand bergs emerge from Greenland's glacial cradle every year. About one percent survive the journey to open water (aka "Iceberg Alley," off the coast of Newfoundland), ready to wreak havoc on the shipping lanes between Europe and North America.

Icebergs are grouped into categories according to size, from the little growlers (three feet high) to the charmingly named "bergy bits" (three to thirteen feet) to the very large specimens running to 250 feet or more, of which roughly seven-eighths lies below the waterline. The largest recorded Arctic "sail," or portion visible above the sea, was 550 feet. The ice itself is also rated on a scale that ranges from Ih and Ic—ordinary ice densities—to Ice IX, X, XI, and XII, all super-cooled lab products. In *Cat's Cradle* (1963), novelist Kurt Vonnegut conjures up a mad scientist bent on formulating the seed for *"ice-nine*—a crystal as hard as this desk—with a melting point of, let us say, . . . one hundred and thirty degrees." The twist is that a mere sliver of ice-nine could congeal all the water on earth in an instant. "When it fell, [rain] would freeze into hard little hobnails of *ice-nine*—and that would be the end of the world!"

> **ICE-T**, aka Tracy Marrow, is a rapper-turned-actor starring in the *Law and Order: Special Victims Unit* prime-time series on NBC television. The father of "gangsta" rap, he recorded hits that include a number called "Cop Killer." His band was known as Body Count. *Ice* was the hip-hop term for "cool" in L.A. in the '80s. Rappers were "ice." Guys in great clothes were "iced." "Man, that car is ice," and so on.

In light of the current concern for global warming, Vonnegut's link between ice and the apocalypse seems less far-fetched. Icebergs, in particular, seem to be the canaries in the coal mine, signaling rapid climatic change. If the great global reservoirs of ice and cold begin to disappear, as Al Gore's Oscar-winning documentary, *An Inconvenient Truth* (2006), contends, sea levels will rise and planetary warming will increase, with dire consequences. The Canadian Ice Service raised the alarm in August 2005 when a forty-one-square-mile shelf of ice in the Arctic Ocean—it had been there for three thousand years—abruptly broke away from Ellesmere Island and headed for open water. This über-berg from the Ayles Ice Shelf, some one hundred feet thick, was trapped by pack ice thirty miles from its point of origin, but the rupture itself provided fresh evidence of an ecological crisis in progress.

In general, however, the Antarctic ice shield, which is larger and colder than its counterpart at the North Pole, generates the majority of truly immense icebergs. By some estimates, 90 percent of the ice locked in bergs is to be found in Antarctica. And a great portion of that ice was contained in the B-15 iceberg, calved from the seventy-five-thousand-year-old Ross Ice Shelf on March 17, 2000. Following reports of a major ice "event," satellite photos taken on March 20 disclosed a flat, tabular iceberg the size of Connecticut—roughly 4,500 square miles—gradually pulling away from shore. At that moment, before fracturing into several smaller units, it was the largest moving object on Earth, easily seen from space with the naked eye.

A team dispatched by *National Geographic* raced to the area in January 2001 to study B-15 and its own calves, eventually landing a helicopter on a massive fragment designated B-15b. The most thrilling part of the expedition came later, however, when the exploration vessel anchored itself to a massive grounded berg near Cape Hallett to conduct an underwater survey of the rich biota sheltered by its underbelly. Suddenly, during the night after the first dives, the iceberg exploded. One end shot into the air, like the prow of a sinking liner, and it plummeted into the depths before the crew's disbelieving eyes, leaving behind shattered ice crystals and a flotilla of bergy bits. Satellite pictures continued to show developing rifts in the ice shelves of Greenland and Antarctica, sending high-risk adventurers into a frenzy of activity. Apart from space travel, iceberg-hopping became the ultimate test of hubris.

> Ice caves produced by glacial melting, volcanic action, or water freezing at great depth are to be found around the globe, from New Mexico, the Pacific Northwest, and New York State to Antarctica, Latin America, and Eastern Europe. The Eisriesenwelt in Austria is **THE LARGEST ICE CAVE** in the world. The site was known to hunters before 1850 but was only officially "discovered" by a scientist in the 1870s. It was developed as a tourist attraction in the 1920s with the addition of carved pathways and wooden planks and railings; more recently, a cable car to the entrance was installed.

The first written description of an iceberg came from St. Brendan of Ireland, who ventured across the Atlantic with several companions in the sixth century (or so he said) in a boat made of cowhide stretched over willow basketry. The monk was especially taken with icebergs or "floating crystal castles" and "columns rising out of the sea," as he described them, harder than marble and silvery in sheen. He spoke from firsthand knowledge about the hardness, since he had rowed for three days to catch up with one pierced through with an arch or cavern. Suffused with the light of a sunset, the great hollow orb seemed to watch over the monks like the eye of God himself. Why not sail through the hole, Brendan asked. And lived to tell all about it. When others, less skillful with the pen, saw what he had seen drifting northward past the Faroe Islands, they told their own stories of icebergs, culminating in the Nordic legends of sea monsters and a region of uncanny apparitions in the Western Ocean.

Iceboating

ICEBOATING, or sailing on what its enthusiasts call "hard water," was first illustrated in a 1605 Dutch engraving showing a square-rigged sailing vessel mounted on runners, like giant skates. The first recorded American iceboat was built in 1790 for a Mr. Southwick of Poughkeepsie, New York. A boxy contraption on skates, it was a practical means of transporting goods across the frozen Hudson River in the wintertime. Only in the 1850s did the standard form of the sleek, recreational iceboat evolve: a cross-shaped backbone and a plank. Iceboating suddenly became a favorite form of winter sport in the old Dutch communities bordering the Hudson and Long Island's ponds. In both locations, ice yacht clubs sprang up.

M. J. Burns, *Ice-yachting on the Hudson, Harper's Weekly,* February 10, 1883

The iceboat became popular in the Midwest in the early 1870s. In 1874, a German shipbuilder who had been launching iceboats in Madison, Wisconsin, for twenty years set up shop on Lake Mendota and developed his own "Madison style," smaller than the Hudson River version with a tiller aft and a triangular body. But it was the 1876 Philadelphia Exposition that made iceboating into a major, competitive activity for the wealthy, like coaching or sea yachting. A new boat displayed by George Buckhout of Poughkeepsie with a cockpit, a sloop's rigging, and a stabilizing runner plank extending far beyond the craft's frame revolutionized the nascent sport.

One of the largest of these new, improved boats was the *Icicle*, owned by James Roosevelt of Hyde Park, father of future president Franklin Roosevelt. Sixty-nine feet long and carrying one thousand square feet of sail, she was the undisputed champion of the Hudson River fleet made famous by engravings in *Harper's Weekly* and other publications of the era. In 1871, *Icicle* won a famous side-by-side race along the river against the "Empire State Express," the fastest train on the New York Central line, at speeds of more than sixty miles per hour. (A modern-day Wisconsin boat—a "Skeeter" type—has been clocked by police radar at 155 mph.)

Tiny, rudderless ice scooters, steered by a pole or jib, may have been invented by fishermen on the south side of Long Island in colonial times. Around 1900, scootering also became a sport with organized race meets and clubs.

In Minnesota, Lake Pepin on the Mississippi and Lakes Miltona and Ida—both near Alexandria—continue to attract the iceboating community whenever "hard water" sets up for the winter.

There is hardly a polar narrative thereafter which does
not include a dramatic scene of a ship "nipped" by the ice,
crushed, or otherwise mangled as strangled screams ema-
nate from bergs trapped in the floe and former landmarks
abruptly appear and disappear like monsters prowling the
endless night. Ernest Shackleton's *Endurance* went to the
bottom under such an attack by ice. Charles Francis Hall's
Polaris was swallowed up, too, in 1871 in a scene of sheer
horror, after Hall himself died of poisoning by person or

Drama on the ice, 1899

persons unknown. Was he done in by an ice monster or an evil spirit trapped on a grounded berg? In 1914, Vilhjalmur Stefansson's *Karluk* and her company were shipwrecked by errant icebergs in mid-ocean, high above the Arctic Circle (whereupon the expedition's leader abruptly took his leave).

Nantucket whalers of the nineteenth century in their frail wooden ships battled monsters of the deep in two forms: either whales or icebergs could stave in a hull without a moment's notice. The *Essex,* the probable model for the climax of Herman Melville's *Moby-Dick* (1851), became a legend when she sank in the Pacific in the winter of 1820, victim of a malevolent sperm whale. Other vessels suffered the same fate during unexpected encounters with icebergs on the Pacific side of the Arctic Ocean. Seven New England whaleboats were rammed by ice and destroyed during the 1851 season alone, as the fleet pushed farther and farther north above the seventieth parallel, where their prey had fled for refuge from the death-dealing harpoons. Were corset stays and fine candles worth the price the whalers paid?

Moby-Dick; or, The Whale, a masterpiece of nineteenth-century American literature, is not much concerned with icebergs, although they lurk at the edges of Melville's story, waiting to pounce on weary lookouts chasing "their game in those frigid Polar Seas, on the very coasts of . . . Esquimaux country." That short passage gave Rockwell Kent, Melville's most important twentieth-century illustrator, license to conjure up a brilliant scene of sailing ships sandwiched between a school of mighty whales in the foreground, their flukes crashing into the waves, and a triad of pinnacled icebergs in the rear, blocking off all means of escape. In Kent's own polar scenes based upon his travels in Alaska and Greenland, icebergs and the mountains echoing their shapes are a kind of leitmotif, a colophon for the rigors and beauties of the far North. But they also hint at a deeper truth about *Moby-Dick:* that in its whiteness, otherworldliness, and omnipresent wrath the whale is, for all intents and purposes, identical to an immense iceberg lurking just outside the field of vision, waiting to stave in the *Pequod* and destroy Ahab's world. One of Melville's poems, "The Berg (A Dream)," describes a warship crushed by an iceberg of invincible animal force, "exhaling still thy dankish breath."

Like an iceberg seen through the eyes of a whaler devoid of literary aspirations, the whale is simply, terribly white. The most challenging chapter of *Moby-Dick* is a meditation on "The Whiteness of the Whale." White—the white of the poles, says Melville—stands for whatever is pure and sublime, as the Romantic poets would have it. Yet there "lurks an elusive something in the innermost idea of this hue, which strikes more of panic to the soul than that redness which affrights in the blood. This elusive quality it is, which causes the thought of whiteness, when divorced from more kindly associations, and coupled with any object terrible in itself, to heighten that terror to the furthest bounds." The polar bear. Coleridge's albatross. A funeral shroud. The "lean ice-monuments" of the Antarctic seas as they appear to the shipwrecked sailor. The iceberg. "And of all these things the Albino Whale was the symbol."

One of Frederic Tudor's captains, short of ice on the outbound leg of a summertime voyage to the tropics in 1912, casually turned north toward Labrador and hacked a few hunks from a passing iceberg. The chopping unbalanced the berg. It upended and rolled over, cutting a long gash in the side of the aptly named *Retrieve*. This time, thanks to round-the-clock pumping, the vessel survived. But earlier that year, on April 14, 1912, the *Titanic* had not been so lucky. As the chorus of the old camp song mournfully declares, "It was sa-ad when the great ship went down / To the bottom." Lives lost: 1,523. Moby-Dick, in the guise of an iceberg, had struck again.

In the bright light of aftersight, it is easy to spot signs of a disaster in the making. A near-collision with a lesser passenger vessel in Southampton as *Titanic* embarked on her maiden voyage. Bruce Ismay, managing director of the White Star Line, who spent most of the fatal day with the latest warning of ice ahead crumpled in his pocket, urging the captain to keep up the speed anyway. Even stranger omens: an obscure 1898 novel called *Futility* about a giant "unsinkable" luxury liner, patronized by the rich and wrecked by an iceberg on a cold April night. But in 1912, *Titanic* was the largest ship the world had ever seen, nine hundred feet long, built in Belfast by the best shipwrights, with a hull made of twenty-six thousand tons of steel. She was fitted out with every amenity. A Louis Quinze–style lounge for the pleasure of the first-class passengers, with hand-carved paneling and replicas of classical statuary. A swimming pool. A Turkish bath done in hand-laid mosaic tile. A massive glass dome over the main staircase. And four raking funnels (one added for purely aesthetic reasons) painted in a brilliant gold. Things were perhaps less plush on the lower decks, in the second-class and steerage quarters, but the ship was, as advertised, more than the largest man-made thing afloat. It was also a miracle of modern technology, double-hulled, protected by a series of watertight compartments for added safety. *Titanic* was, in a word, unsinkable. One of the survivors remembered a kindly deckhand reassuring her that "God Himself could not sink this ship."

Thanks to three feature-length movies, a library's-worth of books, camp songs, and recent expeditions to the wreckage on the ocean floor, everybody knows the story, with its cast of heroes and villains, of how *Titanic* plowed at full speed into an ice field on the Grand Banks despite telegraphed warnings from all sides. At 11:40 on a Sunday evening, lookouts were startled by an iceberg looming darkly in the still waters immediately ahead. The calm ocean may have made a floating obstacle impossible to spot at night. Under normal conditions, white foaming waves at the base of the ice are the best signal of danger. But the temperature had dropped precipitously: that was often a sign of ice. And some crew members, with experience in the North Atlantic, thought they could smell icebergs in the vicinity. Despite frantic evasive maneuvers from the bridge—the popular Captain Smith was already in bed asleep—the iceberg scraped along the starboard side of the gleaming black hull and sailed off into the darkness, leaving panic, ineptitude, and death in its wake.

> "Ice" is a slang term for **DIAMONDS** or, more particularly, stolen diamonds ("hot ice").

Most of the blame in the American press would be heaped on the White Star Line and Director Ismay, who had managed to clamber into a lifeboat despite the "women and children only" rule of the sea. British regulations, it seemed, allowed *Titanic* to sail with lifeboats and collapsible vessels capable of holding only 1,178 lucky souls, although the ship that night carried more than 2,200. A lack of training for the maiden voyage meant that crew members struggled to launch the boats; more important, passengers flatly refused to believe they were in any danger aboard the greatest ship ever built. Even women and children had to be herded, cajoled, or finally tossed into lifeboats. Stories of heroic deeds, most of them questionable, starred titans of industry who shepherded their ladies into the boats and nonchalantly smoked their cigars as the *Titanic* took her final plunge. Foreign-born immigrants and lesser specimens of humanity were, on the contrary, accused of craven cowardice, acts of violence, and a general failure to behave as gentlemen. Class distinctions—and the fact that the American rich were the period's only genuine celebrities—colored the sob stories cranked out to order in the days and weeks following the tragedy.

> Endurance swimmers take a perverse delight in diving into frigid water, and photographers are usually on hand to record the event. These swimmers always smile, unlike the screaming members of Polar Bear Clubs, who plunge through the ice on New Year's Day in major cold-weather cities. In recent years, a British daredevil spent nineteen minutes in the waters of the geographic North Pole—the first human being to do so—in **THE COLDEST WATER EVER ENDURED BY A HUMAN.** Or so he said. Afterward, he grinned while holding onto a tiny iceberg.

So what was it like, the iceberg that struck the *Titanic?* Above water it may not have been impressive, although in survivors' hysterical testimony it grew into a behemoth more than three hundred feet tall. As it scooted past with hardly a whisper, tons of ice bits scattered themselves on the starboard deck. Passengers who were still awake skated about in full evening dress, picking up pieces for their cocktails. A buyer for Gimbels Department Store woke up when fragments shot into his cabin from an open porthole. Later, an inventive liar claimed to have ridden a piece of that iceberg right off the ship and into the water, without so much as getting his trousers wet. But nobody actually got a good look at the rogue iceberg.

On the morning of April 15, as *Carpathia* steamed toward the site summoned by the first SOS signal ever keyed (or not: the story is an enduring part of the *Titanic* myth), the officers observed in the vicinity of the bobbing lifeboats a score of huge bergs, some of them reaching 250 feet into the air, glowing pink and mauve in the predawn light. But most of the infamous *Titanic* iceberg lay beneath the surface when the collision occurred. Several highly publicized submersible expeditions to the hulk of the ruptured vessel since 1986, when Robert Ballard became the first to see *Titanic* since 1912, have fueled speculation about exactly how she foundered. A group of scavengers who looted the debris field in 1987 claimed that one of the immense boilers must have exploded, adding even greater value to the chunks of coal they were selling to souvenir lovers.

Several recent TV specials hosted by the History Channel asked questions about possible structural defects in the rivets or steel plates, rendered brittle by the cold. Or a faulty expansion joint. Or a buckled keel. After all the evidence had been sifted, however, scientists, divers, and buffs alike agreed that the underwater portion of the berg brought down the *Titanic* by squeezing along her starboard flank until the hull burst its rivets and the plates separated, allowing water to flood the ship through a two-hundred-foot gap. The result was inevitable. One after another of the "waterproof" compartments flooded when the sea poured over their internal doors—and the great ship went to the bottom in two immense pieces, in fewer than three hours. An albino whale sank the *Pequod.* A great white beast, rising from the depths, brought down the *Titanic.*

And what did the fatal iceberg look like? Nobody knows. The chief steward on the liner *Prinze Adelbert,* which passed through the general area of the tragedy on Monday, April 15, took a photograph of a berg marked across its base with a red line, indicating possible contact with a vessel. The captain of *Minia,* a ship chartered by White Star to search for bodies in the water, also took a picture of the only big berg in the vicinity of the floating wreckage. A Bohemian seaman, Stephan Rehorek, later claimed to have photographed *Titanic*'s nemesis from the deck of the German steamer *Bremen* five days after the disaster. All the bergs in the photos look lethal enough, but the likelihood that one hunk of ice would have circled the scene for days on end, waiting to be documented, is not great.

Stephan Rehorek, iceberg that sank the Titanic, 1912

Over the years, crackpots have insisted that ice had nothing to do with it: Jews sank the *Titanic!* Or Jesuits! Most of
us believe otherwise. A Welsh gentleman interviewed by the
BBC shortly after James Cameron's blockbuster movie was
released in 1997 was inspired to build a *Titanic*-scale replica
from blueprints lent by the film company. Made entirely of
matchsticks, the nineteen-foot-long ship was accompanied
by an eight-foot iceberg and a patch of ocean crafted of the
same unlikely materials. Less than halfway through the process, he had already used a million matches.

   The most immediate result of the *Titanic* incident was
an international conference held in London in 1913 which
set up the International Ice Patrol, funded by seafaring nations whose ships pass through the North Atlantic during
the ice season. Since then, bergs have been variously shot
at, lassoed, and diverted around stationary oil rigs. Before
World War II, American cutters patrolled the sea-lanes looking for bergs. Since the 1940s, from March through June, air
reconnaissance and GPS devices have charted the "Limit of
All Known Ice." In 1959, a steamship on her maiden voyage
hit an iceberg south of Greenland, just outside the zone, and
sank with ninety-five people on board. But the *Hans Hedtoft*
event was an anomaly. Where more than two thousand big
bergs a year once routinely drifted below 48°N, fewer and
fewer decorate the charts today. Has the Atlantic grown too
hot for them, thanks to global warming? Or, just as the great
whales once fled north to avoid their pursuers, have the great
icebergs found a refuge high in the Arctic in the aftermath of
the 1912 incident that changed the Western world?

   Before *Titanic* sank, technology was an unmixed bless-
ing, a cause for optimism and faith in progress. The rich

were wonderful. The poor were to be shunned. Afterward, with the advent of mechanized warfare in the trenches of World War I, it became possible to wonder if technology was wholly benign after all. *Titanic* failed. So had France's impregnable defenses. (So, in the end, had Frankenstein's great invention.) In addition, war profiteers dimmed the luster of the wealthy; the army threw men and women of all ranks and stations together for the duration, like nervous passengers in one of *Titanic*'s lifeboats. And ordinary men and women—not just business tycoons and society matrons—performed heroic acts. The world turned upside down the night *Titanic* met her fatal iceberg.

There is some cockeyed disaster-porn thrill to be derived from the thought that the average glass of tap water, the ice cube in every Coke, still contains molecules from the iceberg that laid low the great ship. Nature has had her way. The wreckage of the *Titanic* has all but dissolved into ghastly tendrils of rust floating in the ice-cold darkness, two miles below the surface.

7

EXHIBITING ICE AND ICE PEOPLE

"Of these death-white regions I formed an idea of my own"

—

Charlotte Bronte, *Jane Eyre* (1847)

 The earth's secrets have been pretty well laid bare in the twenty-first century. Satellites, airplanes, and TV specials have encouraged tourism by proxy. The all-seeing camera goes; the traveler stays home with beer and pizza. The once-heroic profession of explorer has been replaced by packaged thrill seeking. The Scotts and the Pearys, with their pemmican and tea, went to the poles in search of chilly thrills, too, but they cloaked their ambitions in the mantle of science. And if nothing else, they filled in the last blank spaces on the map. To swim over the magnetic North Pole in a Speedo in temperatures that killed the unlucky castaways from the *Titanic* (as one British daredevil recently did) takes a full support team and a bevy of publicists. To climb Mount Everest today with a retinue of professional guides and cell phones might (and does) have its dangers, but there is little chance that the modern adventurer will find something new up there—unless the Yeti is real. Through the World War II era, however, most people still had only the haziest vision of what farthest North—along with its resident populations of wildlife and humans—looked like. About the farthest South, they knew even less.

The Antarctic has been a *tabula rasa* throughout most of human history. The legendary Captain James Cook, dispatched by the British Admiralty to learn if there was anything but more ocean down there—the "Terra Australis" or

Lewis Gordon Pugh after a nineteen-minute swim at the North Pole, 2007

seventh continent shown on an ancient Ptolemaic map—set forth in the HMS *Resolution* in 1774–75, found unimaginable quantities of ice, and circumnavigated Antarctica without ever actually seeing it. In 1819, the Czar of Russia sent out another mission, which seems to have officially "discovered" Antarctica at a distance on January 28, 1820. At the end of the same year an enterprising American seal boat captained by Nathaniel B. Palmer unequivocally sighted land. But none of the pioneer navigators were foolish enough to attempt a landing. Certainly no one pined to stay there until ten members of a British expedition wintered over intentionally on Cape Adare in 1900, setting off the international frenzy to find the pole at any cost.

Antarctica is still not truly inhabited by human beings: scientists, a few artists, and support staff at its scattered research stations rotate through for limited periods of time, acutely aware of the dangers of an empty terrain occupied only by ice and perpetual danger. Even emergency evacuations are often impossible. Dr. Jeri Nielsen, on sabbatical at the Amundsen-Scott station, became the news story of the year in 1999 after she performed a biopsy on her own cancerous breast and self-administered chemotherapy during the March to October blackout period for aircraft landings. The event quickly became a book and a TV movie-of-the-week, giving stay-at-homes a vicarious taste of the hazards of trying to live a normal life at the South Pole.

> **"THE ICEMAN"** is the deserved nickname of Wim Hof, an extreme sports enthusiast from the Netherlands whose feats include holding his breath under polar ice for six minutes and running a half marathon barefoot on ice and snow. He has also climbed Mount Everest in shorts, traversing the "Death Zone" above twenty-six thousand feet, where an unknown number of dead mountaineers lie crumpled on the trail, frozen and desiccated by the extreme cold. Sometimes they are mistaken for logs and rocks by weary climbers looking for a place to sit down.

Those dangers are ramped up another notch in John Carpenter's landmark horror movie *The Thing* (1982), set at a remote Antarctic research station meticulously copied from official government photos of the Amundsen-Scott installation as it then appeared. Twelve men live there as the movie begins. The only female is the voice on a clunky chess-playing computer used by Kurt Russell, a hard-drinking, macho loner whose isolation from the group allows him to see that something is amiss in Antarctica. And that something is *the* Thing, an agile shape-shifter from outer space with a special talent: if a single slimy, rage-filled cell of thingness enters a host body, it kills off the normal cells and replaces them with its own (just like cancer). In short order, the nearby Norwegian station is rubbed out and the Americans can no longer tell which of their number has been turned into a Killer Alien.

In a less philosophical way, *The Thing* toys with the Frankenstein dilemma: what does it mean to be human? On another level, it strips away the inessential essentials, like heat and sleep and nourishment, to ask the question in the starkest possible terms. Nothing and absence become the settings for the drama as well as an imaginative portrait of Antarctica—where "Man is the warmest place to hide!" In the mental landscape, Antarctica is vacancy. It is blurry hundred-year-old photos of tiny Euro-Americans foiled off against mountainous heaps of ice, and it is modern ones showing spectacular glaciers and bergs and only occasionally a few figures in high-tech red snowsuits lost against an ice field that trails off forever. The alternative is the Antarctic of *The March of the Penguins* (2005), the hit documentary in which the only human thing is the narrator's voice describing a year in the life of a flock of penguins careening from natural disaster to natural catastrophe.

The Arctic was easier to imagine. Europeans had ventured into northern waters regularly since the Middle Ages. Folktales offered additional clues about what might be found there. From the moment word circulated that Columbus had located a land barrier between the Atlantic Ocean and the Orient, artists rushed into print pictures based on sailors' stories of the wonders they had seen. Even William Shakespeare's *The Tempest* (1611–12), with its monstrous Caliban, alludes to the strange creatures to be encountered in the New World. But the northern reaches of America, where openings in the ice hinted at the existence of an elusive Northwest Passage between the seas, quickly became the focus for Old World nations in search of wealth and expanded trade. And from there, locked in the ice for years on end, Europeans bent on finding that passage to China sent back word of a group of symbols that came to define the Arctic of the popular imagination. Mirages. Ice and icebergs, the latter often spotted thanks to "ice blink," a reflection of the frozen surface on the face of the clouds. Eerie silence, broken only by the thunderous explosions of the pack ice and the ominous moans of wooden ships pinched by moving floes. Violent storms. Bitter cold. Smiling, fur-clad "Esquimaux," as the native population was almost universally described. And igloos, of course: domical Eskimo huts made of ice—or was it snow?—demonstrating a great technical ingenuity among the most "primitive" specimens of mankind yet encountered.

> The Internet is a rich source for step-by-step directions on how to construct an igloo in your backyard. Because warmth builds up inside the structure, ice forms on the dome's exterior. So, in a cold climate, homemade igloos can easily last the season. **"ESKIMOLD"** kits include a tub for molding snow into blocks of the proper size and a plastic snow knife, all for about twenty-four dollars. Other companies, ranging from Target on the low end to Hammacher Schlemmer on the high end, market semi-inflatable vinyl igloos for folks who are ice shy.

ARCTIC REGIONS!

WILL OPEN ON MONDAY, MARCH 3d,
AT THE

ASSEMBLY BUILDINGS
Corner Tenth and Chesnut Streets.

DR. E. BEALE'S
GRAND ILLUMINATED HISTORY OF
American, English and Danish Explorations
IN SEARCH OF

Sir JOHN FRANKLIN
IN THE

FRIGID ZONE.
Embracing a complete Voyage from New York to the North Pole.

In connection with which, will also be exhibited the Siege and Bombardment of

SEBASTOPOL,
Giving an entire view of the City and environs;

Together with all the different Fleets & Armies

GEORGE HEILGE, Esq., OF PHILADELPHIA,

The Panorama will be accompanied by an appropriate and explanatory Lecture,

By Prof. D. C. Larue, of New York.

RECOMMENDATION—READ! READ!!

EXHIBITIONS EVERY EVENING AT HALF-PAST 7 O'CLOCK, AND ON
Wednesday and Saturday Afternoons at 3 o'clock

Admission, 25 Cents.   Children under 12 Years, Half-Price

Newspaper notice of
panorama show, 1856

These stereotypes persisted almost unaltered for four centuries, while the polar ice cap melted, the First Nations peoples of the north—the Inuit—were identified and provided with a written history, and the Northwest Passage was conquered by the nuclear-powered submarines and massive icebreakers of the aptly named Cold War. A good index of the survival of this limited range of polar imagery is *Tom Swift in the Caves of Ice* (ca. 1911), an adventure book for American boys, part of a famous syndicate-produced series issued under the pen name of Victor Appleton. Tom, whose forté is modern mechanisms, sets out for Alaska and beyond in an airship. "Off for the frozen North!" he cries as he speeds away in search of a "valley of gold" dimly recalled by an old miner. The farther he goes, the more terrible the storms, the thicker the ice. Even the mountains are so thickly frosted "as to resemble the great bergs that float in the polar sea." Natives appear. Their dwellings are fashioned from "blocks of ice." Indeed, in the valley of gold, a series of natural caverns hollowed out of the ice resemble igloos built on a far larger scale. But when the ice field unexpectedly breaks up and drifts out to sea, the gold is lost. So is the airship. Tom is rescued from the cold by friendly Eskimos, builds an igloo of his own, and eventually finds his way home, poorer but wiser in the ways of the North. During the first golden age of the illustrated news magazine in the mid-nineteenth century, penny papers were full of black-and-white wood engravings affording tantalizing glimpses of what a modern generation of explorers was seeing above the Arctic Circle. The period's often-repeated iconography included the mysterious arc of the aurora borealis, cliffs of ice of impossible height, and the usual complement of very small ships, igloos, and teams of British or American naval personnel man-hauling heavy sledges across featureless white plains. Desirable also were Europeanized portraits of Eskimos (especially the women) showing mothers with babies, strange hairstyles, and peculiar costumes. Often explorers "went native," at least for the press, having themselves depicted in full northern regalia, quite unlike the woolens they had persisted in wearing. The Earl of Lonsdale, for example, capped off an 1888–89 sporting expedition to the Canadian north by posing for a San Francisco photographer in furs and mukluks or *kamik*, an enormous pair of snowshoes by his side. Turned into an engraving, the portrait appeared in an 1890 issue of the *Illustrated London News.* In America, *Harper's Illustrated Weekly* carried the same kinds of iconic images.

The most influential pictures of the Arctic, however, came in the form of panoramas. These extremely long paintings were of two varieties. One type was mounted around the 360-degree circumference of a specially built "rotunda."

Customers presented their tickets and walked inside, where they found themselves entirely surrounded by Arctic scenery. The Messrs. Marshall of Glasgow, who toured Britain and the continent with their "New Peristrephic Panorama of the Sublime Scenery of the Frozen Regions" in the 1830s, were showmen. They had engaged teams of artists, or so the ads said, to crank out ten thousand square feet of faithful renderings based on sketches made by two officers and "Saccheuse the Esquimaux" on an 1818 expedition to find the elusive Northwest Passage. It was all there, according to the breathless copy: "Icebergs, islands of Ice, . . . [and] Manners and Costumes of the Natives, &c." And, as if all that were not enough, a military band had been engaged to play throughout. Under gaslight, viewers were also invited to inspect a collection of polar curiosities, including Saccheuse's own boat (a kayak?), a live sled dog, and a stuffed polar bear. Patrons were slyly advised that "the Frozen Regions are always rendered a comfortable temperature by Stoves."

A second type of panorama consisted of a long roll of canvas slowly unwound across a stage, in the manner of the later motion picture, with a take-up reel concealed behind the curtains. As scenes glided by in continuous motion, the impresario described in florid detail what the audience was seeing. Frequently, the pictorial action was supplemented by offstage sound effects of growling bears and crashing ice. The result was a spectacle, rendered informative and educational by association with a famous name. In the United States, Elisha Kent Kane's search for the lost Franklin expedition spawned no fewer than four panoramas, each of which traveled with its own sideshows of relics ranging from Kane himself in wax effigy to a stuffed husky sled dog and the actual boat in which Kane had escaped when his ship was nipped in the ice. Once assembled and booked, these shows toured until the paint wore off the canvas. In 1864, Frederic Church, whose gigantic iceberg painting was currently on tour, had to skip a planned exhibition-for-pay in Philadelphia because one of several Kane panoramas— "the largest ever painted," according to its owner—would have siphoned off business.

Panoramas were not limited to Arctic subject matter. Like newsreels, they unfurled pictorial confirmation of whatever was current or memorable, from exploration to natural disasters, from train wrecks to the palace of Versailles and the battles of the Civil War. The visual aspect of the panorama appealed particularly to illiterates; because the price of admission was cheaper than the cost of books or magazines, they also answered the needs of the urban poor. As a phenomenon, they fascinated a century that found its own doings of primary interest. Charles Dickens invented a comic character named Mr. Booley, a world traveler who had visited the upper reaches of the Mississippi and the icebergs of Baffin Bay without ever leaving London, thanks to panoramas. Mark Twain poked fun at the spectacles, too—especially the zippy and often inappropriate musical numbers without which no panorama was complete.

Man in front of panorama, ca. 1850s

The logical next step in the evolution of Arctic shows was to introduce live explorers and the natives they "discovered." People from the far North had been displayed as novelties or "savages" in England as early as 1501. But the age of exploration ushered in a new desire for authentic experience. Elisha Kent Kane, after his homecoming in 1855, went on the lecture circuit swaddled in furs. Charles Hall toured with an Inuit family brandishing their bows and arrows and spears and a pack of barking dogs that joined him onstage at the end of his performances. Although this particular group of Westernized Esquimaux had already met Queen Victoria before Hall plucked them off a dock on Baffin Island, he dressed them in sealskin suits—and delighted crowds by having them answer questions from the floor in impeccable English.

Eventually one of the Inuit died and the other two fell ill, after stints in sideshows and at P. T. Barnum's New York museum. And while Hall spoke of their ingenuity and "positiveness," human exhibitions like his exploited the exoticism—the primitivism—of the people of the North. They were human curiosities, on a par with sled dogs and Franklin relics. Esquimaux on display seemed all the stranger to Americans of the day because of the poverty of their material culture and because, after the Civil War, swift industrial "progress" highlighted the state of human beings still supposedly living in a kind of perpetual Stone Age. A crude picture ad in the New York Times in November 1862 showed Hall's Eskimo family standing on a sheet of ice in front of an igloo village surrounded by a forest of icebergs: "Only Three Days More," and then they were to be replaced by a family of albinos, performing bears from California, and "life likenesses of Queen Victoria and the Prince of Wales." While all that was going on, Ebierbing, Tookoolite, the baby, and the backdrop of igloos were being loaned out by Hall for public exhibition in Boston.

Like Knute, the much-publicized orphan polar bear raised by a keeper at the Berlin Zoo in 2006 and 2007, Eskimos were wildly popular in the 1800s because they seemed cute and harmless. And because they were a marker of just how far true civilization had come. Knute inspired the sale of stuffed bears by the carload to parents and children with no real conception of what a wild animal was like. Dr. Frederick Cook, before he was discredited for claiming to have beaten Peary to the "Big Nail" (the North Pole), did a brisk business in dolls dressed in fur outfits and little toy sleds. Peary's journals are full of plans to market a "Peary North Pole" sled for children and commemorative snowshoes

Dr. Vilhjalmur Stefansson, early twentieth-century Arctic explorer, promoted the use of igloos.

with ivory mounts, to be sold by male and female clerks in native costume. Spectacle was big business, and spectacle translated readily into toys, dime novels, cigar bands, trading cards, and thrilling dramas.

Kane's Arctic exploits of 1853–55 became a play almost as soon as he arrived back on American soil. The most interesting of the nineteenth-century polar dramas, however, was written in 1857 by Wilkie Collins, with a verse prelude by Charles Dickens. Furthermore, Dickens played the villain in *The Frozen Deep*, took a passionate interest in every aspect of the elaborate production, and eventually staged the play at his own home, where amateur Christmas theatricals on a huge scale had become a holiday tradition. He ordered a panorama's worth of authentic props and costumes, manufactured paper snow to be scattered on cue by a cadre of "snowboys," and staged a spectacle of his own so famous that he eventually presented his prologue for Queen Victoria during a command performance.

A great fan of adventure stories when he was a boy, Dickens was roused to action in the case of *The Frozen Deep* by the published reports of Dr. John Rae, who had first joined the search for the Franklin party in 1848. Several years later, scouring King William Land for clues to their whereabouts, he met Inuit hunters who possessed Franklin artifacts and told a strange tale of dying white men, madness, and cannibalism. Rae subsequently wrote a summary of his findings, concluding on the basis of human bones he examined in 1854 (and the remains of a dubious stew frozen in the bottom of a kettle) that corpses had been dismembered and eaten as the last scurvy-ridden survivors fought their way toward safety. Dickens, the editor of *Household*

Words, was appalled by the suggestion and, in a pair of essays printed in his own weekly, denied that any such thing had occurred.

The crux of Dickens's case was that natives could simply not be trusted. Moreover, it was inconceivable that his polar heroes could have sunk to such depravity, even in the face of certain death. The articles put Dickens firmly on the side of Lady Franklin and the monarchy during the debate over further polar activity that followed Rae's sensational report. Dickens then reinterpreted the role of Wardour, the villain of Collins's play, to make him struggle against the iciness of his heart, like a true British hero. The stage set, lacking the vastness of the Arctic wastes, was a cabin. When the door was opened, in blew the paper snow as the Union Jack fluttered in the distance.

It was only a short step from stage scenery to the ethnological "villages" of the great world's fairs of the late nineteenth and early twentieth centuries. At the 1876 fair in Philadelphia, held in honor of the national centenary, there were life-size mannequins of an Eskimo man and his wife, part of a vaguely educational exhibit showing the variousness of humankind. But by the time the 1893 fair was mounted in Chicago, in honor of Columbus's voyages to the New World, anthropology and science had made inroads in the popular consciousness. Chicago inherited the "village" concept of re-creating the daily lives of natives from the seminal Paris Exposition of 1889. There, the village was a profitable innovation that neatly contrasted the temporary residents' various huts and yurts with the Eiffel Tower, that wonder of modern hubris, looming 984 feet overhead. Scholars have argued that such villages legitimated the practice of gaping at Filipinos, Native Americans, and Egyptians in native garb. That they provided a welcome distraction from the overre-finement of urban life. That they "commodified the exotic" or justified imperialist ambition. That, to ladies in whalebone corsets and gentlemen in black suits with rolled umbrellas, they demonstrated the triumph of Western sophistication over poorly dressed (or undressed) savagery.

The World's Columbian Exposition, held in Chicago in 1893, contained the first of the Paris-style villages. These displays fell under the jurisdiction of "Department M," directed by Professor Frederick Ward Putnam, a prominent Harvard ethnologist. Putnam gave Department M the veneer of scientific inquiry, but, as the name suggested, the larger part of his domain was the Midway, the fair's giant amusement zone. This put a party of sixty Inuit from Labrador on a par with the Ferris wheel, as they and their dogs sweated through the summer in picturesque fur garments

Inuit group at Columbian Exposition, 1893

under threat that if they took 'em off their grocery deliveries would cease. From the fall day when they arrived on the Lake Michigan site—and their quarters on the northwest corner of the grounds—to acclimate themselves to the hot weather, the Eskimo were a huge hit. Visitors arrived at the impromptu sideshow long before the fair opened and paid a fee to inspect a newborn baby, a chubby brown boy named Christopher Columbus. (Not coincidentally, 1893 was also the year in which Peary's white "Snow Baby" was born in the ice fields of the far North.)

> One of the most famous ice mummies was the **MINNE-SOTA ICEMAN**, the body of a tallish male with very large feet and a nose like that of a Pekingese dog. Covered in thick brown hair, the Iceman was displayed at fairs and carnivals for thirty-five cents a look in the 1960s. The impresario, who kept him on ice in a coffin with a glass lid, claimed that Russian seal hunters found the Iceman floating in a block of sea ice off the coast of eastern Siberia. Zoologists initially pronounced him the find of the century. Then a young woman came forward claiming that this was the beast she had shot dead in the woods near Bemidji, Minnesota, when he assaulted her several months before. But the Iceman was neither the "missing link" nor a murderous "Bigfoot." Further investigation found that he had been fabricated in Hollywood in 1967 by a special effects team attempting to match an artist's conception of a Cro-Magnon man with a broken skull.

Although the Inuit had been promised $100,000 and a load of provisions to take back home with them, conditions in their overcrowded log cabins (a practical alternative to igloos) soon deteriorated. The owners of the Eskimo Village concession, J. W. Skiles and Co. of Spokane, made their profits on the sale of native crafts and the price of admission. On the other side of the turnstile, their charges paddled kayaks around an artificial lake and cracked long whips over unruly dogs. If the Eskimos refused to perform as advertised, receipts dried up. In February, one Inuit grabbed a hired interpreter and shook him angrily, probably over the bad living conditions and the poor food. In April, another malcontent who refused to wear his fur costume during a heat wave was bluntly informed that if he didn't, he would get nothing to eat. The police were called. Five families hired a lawyer and sued the firm and the onsite manager (who had called them "chattels"). Their contract was dissolved by the court. One Eskimo got a job as an exposition carpenter at much higher wages. Others drifted homeward via engagements to tour with one of Cook's shows along the eastern seaboard. Still others, wise in the ways of sideshows, set themselves up in business as human exhibits just outside the fairgrounds, where Indians from Buffalo Bill Cody's Wild West Show pitched their tents. There is no record of serious ethnological studies having been undertaken at the fair.

Minor problems like these did not dampen enthusiasm for villages as leading entertainment attractions, however. The Pan-American Exposition (1901) in Buffalo corralled its own troupe of "slant-eyed" Eskimos and set them up in papier-mâché igloos at the midway entrance. It cost ten cents to take a look or fifteen cents to linger over the various props and artifacts. Trade cards advertising "The Esquimaux in Their Village of Ice" listed the wonders to be found there: "54 genuine sealskin kayaks," three sled teams, six snow igloos—*not* said to be genuine—assorted *topeks* and *komatiks,* and "the only Whalebone Igloo." It was, blared the *Buffalo Express*, "the best educational feature on the Midway."

Health issues arose in the village during the fair's run: eleven cases of measles, the death of a baby, pneumonia, a quarantine. The twenty-four Eskimos brought from Nome, Alaska, on a Norwegian vessel along with members of two other unrelated tribes always craved ice. W. G. Taber, the concessionaire, was heard to scold his cast for swimming (without parkas) in the "polar sea" in front of their igloos.

Otherwise, their stint in Buffalo was uneventful, according to an oral history handed down in the family of "Unaquthlook" or Maryanne, one of the villagers. The Eskimo encampment in Buffalo is memorable, however, because it was recorded on film by Thomas A. Edison, Inc., in 1901, in a seventy-five-foot reel called *Scene in the Esquimaux Village*.

There were actually three scenes, each shot from its own fixed camera position by Edwin S. Porter and James H. White. Taken together, they provide a panoramic view of the village, a plaster and paint creation consisting of a rugged, three-dimensional iceberg background, a large ice cave in which performers could regroup, a pool in front with shorelines that served as a stage, and moveable igloos scattered here and there. One scene shows a complicated game of "Snap the Whip," in which participants snatch nickels from a target with their lashes in front of a pointed tent made of skins. Another shows an equally complicated game of "Leap Frog" or "Misheetak." The last and longest segment shows a footrace on the edge of the pond followed by a sled race over what looks to be a slick pathway of ice and snow. Women and children are not visible. All the performers are grown men in full Eskimo regalia, although the sunlight is brilliant and the performances seem to have been photographed in early summer. In the autumn, President McKinley was assassinated at the Buffalo fair, somewhat dimming fond memories of the Eskimo games.

But as St. Louis geared up for its own world's fair in 1904, honoring the Louisiana Purchase of 1804, the theme of Lewis and Clark's western exploration called for more and better displays of the spoils of American treks to unfamiliar places. Enter the Eskimos. This time, their village was only a stone's throw from one of the most compelling sights on the "Pike" or midway—a large, turreted building modeled on an ice castle, with fake bergs at its base and off to one side a phony ice field in which a brave three-masted vessel sat hopelessly imprisoned. "New York to the North Pole" spoke directly to the public interest in polar explorers with an honor roll of heroes emblazoned on the facade. The British and Norwegians were there, but the list was top-heavy with American names, including Kane, Grinnell, Greely, and Peary.

Beyond the impressive battlements waited a new type of experience, a "simulation ride" perfected at world's fairs and revived a half century later at Disneyland as the "dark ride." Spectators sat in the dark before an expanse of water. Thanks to sound effects and artificial lighting, they witnessed a two-hundred-foot ship, the *Discoverer*, at anchor in New York harbor by moonlight. Gradually it sets sail past the Battery and under the Brooklyn Bridge at dawn and pushes north until, under the eerie glow of the aurora borealis, it is hemmed in by icebergs. In the final scene, the crew dashes for a semitropical North Pole protected by ice and raises the Stars and Stripes, five years before Peary claimed to have done the same. It was almost as good as being there and, in the oppressive heat of a Missouri summer, a lot warmer.

> An *Inukshuk* is a directional marker or guidepost erected by the Inuit in the Canadian Arctic. A variation on the type—an *Inunguak*—resembles a Cubist sculpture of a human figure with widespread arms and legs and is shown on the flag of the Nunavut Territory. It will be the logo for the Vancouver Winter Olympics of 2010. These humanoid stone images occupy hilltops and mark them as places of power. Miniature tourist versions are made of glass to resemble ICE CARVINGS.

The St. Louis Eskimos were housed in one of the most eye-catching buildings in Forest Park—a massive glacier reaching almost one hundred feet into the air and supported by a colonnade of icicles. Here, the tickets went for a quarter but, once in the giant cave hollowed out of ersatz ice, the variety of instructive goings-on was worth the price. The Eskimos were, or seemed to be, complete families, with children and their mothers as active as the men. In addition to the usual sports and games, the usual igloos (many painted on canvas flats hung above the stage area) and lakes, and every other far North stereotype spectators carried in the mind's eye, there were wedding and burial ceremonies conducted at regular intervals and demonstrations of panning for gold nuggets in Alaska. During daily parades on the Pike, small children guiding their own dogsleds were crowd favorites.

So was a veteran exhibition Eskimo, the eleven-year-old "Nancy Columbia," born at the Columbian Exposition of 1893 and featured at every noteworthy fair since, along with her mother, one of Peary's trusted interpreters. The smallest

children spent part of every day in the sandbox on the play-
ground of the Model Street, costumed to the hilt and in the
company of other little folk from Japan, the Middle East, and
other mysterious lands represented at the fair. A symbolic
Thanksgiving dinner chronicled in the St. Louis newspapers

saw an Eskimo girl in a bearskin
robe sharing her turkey with the
daughter of a Cheyenne chief:
the pair represented the am-
ity between all quarters of the
American empire. The organizers had provided twenty-four
turkeys and all the trimmings,
but the little Eskimo girl from
the make-believe igloo inside
the make-believe iceberg liked
the ice cream best. Yet she was

Nancy Columbia with dog at
St. Louis World's Fair, 1904

not quite part of a typical ice-cream-cone-licking St. Louis
family. The jack of clubs in a deck of playing cards issued
as a souvenir of her village shows five Eskimos sitting in a
row in front of their quarters. The women and children on
the left wear their native furs. The young man on the right
sports a suit and tie. The caption reads "Evolution."

8

HOLES IN THE ICE

"The secrets, mysteries and destinies will finally be revealed"

—

Ad for *Pirates of the Caribbean: At World's End* (2007)

 So promised the ads for *Pirates of the Caribbean: At World's End,* one of 2007's multiplex blockbusters, the third in the filmic series starring Johnny Depp as an addled buccaneer with eye shadow and a mincing gait. The plot, as always, is inconsequential. The *Pirates* franchise is all about atmosphere: swordplay, amazing special effects, cheeky dialogue, and lots of ocean. Until this latest sequel, however, the jolly crew had stuck to warm-water ports, as good pirates should. But that summer they sailed off into polar ice, hemmed in by photogenic bergs, until their vessel was abruptly sucked into a maelstrom and ended up in—what? Nirvana? Utopia? A sinless Eden? Certainly not the lair of Frankenstein, the Undead! No. A beautiful, warm, peaceful place, where our heroine

(played by Keira Knightley) will raise her son and await the
periodic return of her dishy lover (Orlando Bloom). Phew!

This is not the first time expanses of ice have evoked
a spine-tingling feeling that *something* must lie below or
beyond the implacable whiteness and cold and desolation.
Long before science discovered vitamin C, many seafarers
believed that scurvy was caused by the dismal, eternal vista
of polar landscapes. Others were convinced that the same
landscapes were simply nature's way of testing humankind's
persistence—that beyond the ice stretched an "Open Polar
Sea" leading to a land of enchantment, or at least a terrain

Hole in the ice, fishing contest, 1955

devoid of scurvy-making ice. Elisha Kane justified a second American expedition in search of the missing Franklin party (1853–55) on the basis of this theory. Since the time of Ptolemy, writers had suggested that open water flowed without interruption around the globe. Mapmakers often pictured tranquil spaces at the top and bottom of Earth. Whalers called such regions of calm, navigable water hidden in the ice *polynia*. On the lecture circuit to promote his venture in 1852, Kane posited that Sir John Franklin and his crew may have fought their way into this open polar sea and were somehow trapped there, unable to find the way back through the ice barrier. At the podium, dressed in his "nannooke" or bearskin breeches, Kane made a plausible case for a kind of Shangri-la of the North, where Franklin still awaited his Yankee saviors.

Isaac Hayes, the surgeon who served the Kane expedition, used scientific goals rather than forlorn hopes of seeing Franklin as the justification for his 1860 voyage to the Arctic. Specifically, Hayes set sail from Boston on a rainy Fourth of July day to find the fabled sea beyond the ice. He managed to plunder Eskimo graves for ethnographic study and to lose several colleagues to hypothermia, exile, and natural causes. And, needless to say, he never did find the open polar sea, although Hayes thought cracks in the ice around Ellesmere Island might indicate that it lay just over the horizon. By the time he limped back into port, the Civil War was more important to Americans than the wanderings of explorers whom the *New York Times* called mere "Lotus-eaters," seduced by dreams of a paradisial ice-free north.

The myth of the open polar sea—the notion that something abnormal and possibly divine lies beyond the ice—appealed mightily to Edgar Allan Poe. Poe's interest in Antarctica was roused by Jeremiah Reynolds, another dashing platform speaker who began agitating for an American expedition to the South Pole in 1825. Poe (who is said to have uttered Reynolds's name on his deathbed) used Terra Australis as the setting for two works. The first, a short story called *MS. Found in a Bottle* (1833), describes a ship blown off course into strange lands. In this case, a galleon manned by a Coleridge-like crew of living dead men skitters toward the pole, only to be drawn through a gap in the ice into a whirlpool. And there the tale ends abruptly, like a true-life report cast up in a bottle on some distant beach.

The second work is a similar hoax, a fearsome story masquerading as fact buttressed by references to the logbooks of famous explorers and the theories of leading polar experts. *The Narrative of Arthur Gordon Pym* (1838) claims to be the fragmentary journal of a Nantucket mariner well versed in the Antarctic literature of his day. He sees some things that subsequent research has determined do not exist: a race of curly-haired white bears, for example, with bulldog snouts and blood red eyes. But beyond the ice floes, beyond the tepid waters of the open polar sea, his ship sails into a chasm and comes out somewhere else altogether, in a mysterious land of large, snow white humanoid inhabitants. And there the narrative breaks off abruptly. A postscript reveals that the final chapters are lost and that Pym has recently died.

The theory that the icy poles protect giant holes (four thousand miles across) leading to hidden inner worlds was promulgated beginning in 1818 by Captain John Cleves Symmes, an ex–frontier officer in the War of 1812. His first "circular" on the subject, published in St. Louis, opens with a bold statement: "I declare the earth is hollow and habitable within; containing a number of solid concentric spheres, one within the other, and that it is open at the poles twelve or sixteen degrees." Put another way, he was insisting that rings of ice and open polar seas formed mere anterooms to what were known as the two "Symmes Holes," one in the far North, the other in Antarctica. The holes led down into the planet's very core, where, as Poe would convincingly demonstrate, worlds both idyllic and horrific awaited the intrepid adventurer.

Symmes's disciple, Jeremiah Reynolds, joined him on the lecture circuit in 1825, dropping the names of legitimate scientists at every stop. Newton, Halley, Humboldt, and Davy were mentioned frequently to bolster the scientific veracity of the theory, as well as ancient texts and the memoirs of those who plied the polar waters in search of seals and whales. Because nobody had actually passed through the ice barrier successfully—excepting Franklin, if he still sailed the open polar sea—Symmes's jerry-rigged notions were just as good as any others. "Symmes Holes" soon became part of the common parlance of the age. Worn out by his exertions, however, Symmes died in 1829 and was buried in Hamilton, Ohio, beneath an obelisk bearing a hollow globe of stone pierced through with openings at the poles. But his legacy lived on into the era of Peary and Amundsen thanks to the writings of Reynolds, Poe, Melville, and possibly Captain Symmes himself. Usually attributed to Symmes but issued under the name of Captain Adam Seaborn, *Symzonia: Voyage of Discovery* (1820) is another Barnum-like hoax, the first American utopian novel, and a "proof" that the ideal societies of hollow earth actually existed.

Symzonia (the name of the land beneath) has also been described as a 248-page ad for Symmes and his theories: he is lavishly praised and cited throughout. In the story of the voyage, his imaginary ship sails though the "icy loop," claims the South Pole for the United States, slips over the edge, and comes upon a warm, beautiful, pastoral place inhabited by short, white, smart, athletic vegetarians who live to the age of two hundred years in a state of democratic bliss. The Symzonians, it develops, are the ancestors of modern mankind. Those who dwell in the gross External World are unhappy exiles from the perfection lying at the bottom of a Symmes Hole.

In a way, the strange folk who populate *Symzonia* and *The Narrative of Arthur Gordon Pym* fed a growing appetite for exotica also expressed in popular fiction: the drama of American, Norwegian, and British teams actually conquering the poles—which did *not* contain holes—merely swelled the audience for Edgar Rice Burroughs's string of lurid hollow earth novels. Often dismissed as six-cents-a-line prose, his six Pellucidar novels beginning with *At the Earth's Core* (1914) owed a debt to Verne's *Journey to the Center of the Earth* (1864). But they were oddly practical, too, full of aspiring coal miners using steam-driven drills to enter an inner sphere with its own sun and a race of gorgeous lizard-like females who turn out to be very bad customers indeed. Tensions over mechanization, women's right to vote, militarism, and all manner of other contemporary ills are thus safely tucked away in a realm of the imagination. The author also posits an inner world younger somehow than our own, a world without human time, in which Stone Age cultures flourish alongside dinosaurs, fabulous underground cities, and, thanks to the avaricious miners, American-style factories. In the 1920s, even Tarzan turns up in this la-la land to do battle with various nonwhite hostiles from prehistory. The illustrations, drawn from Burroughs's circle of friends among Chicago's best advertising artists, were sexy, thrilling, and suitably bizarre.

> Urban legend alert! If you wake up bleeding in a hotel bathroom in a **TUB FILLED WITH ICE CUBES**, you may have fallen victim to a well-organized gang of thieves working high-end hostelries from coast to coast. The object? Kidneys for transplant, with recipients willing to pay thousands for fresh organs. Call 911, say the experts, and sit still until help arrives.

Those who retailed harrowing tales of polar exploration to genteel audiences often spiced up their lectures with live Eskimos in full northern regalia, sled dogs, and relics. Panoramas, "villages," and the apparatus of showmanship in general made use of both scenery and Arctic dwellers, however inaccurately portrayed. It is no secret that many travelers to the North regarded the indigenous populations as savages, primitives, or subhumans—representatives of an earlier Pellucidaran age who had somehow lived on into the modern era thanks to their isolation, just like characters in

Explorer Matthew Henson

a Burroughs novel. After seven failed attempts, Robert Peary of North Pole fame recruited whole villages of Inuit—*his* Eskimo—to make the final push to his goal. Left behind at the moment of glory, Ootah, Egingwah, Ooqueah, and Seegloo remained all but nameless for generations. Their anonymity was matched by that of Matthew Henson, the "servant" whose knowledge of local languages and technologies ensured Peary's success. Only later was this heroic African American written back into the saga of which he had been a vital part. In the minds of Peary and many of his fellow polar pilgrims, those who were not Anglo-Saxon were relegated to the role of sideshow accessories. In retirement on an island off the Maine coast, Peary built himself two Inuit houses, one a "replica of a snow igloo" and the other an igloo "modified for explorer's use." Time and tides subsequently carried away these bits of make-believe scenery for Peary's personal drama of unaided greatness.

Donald MacMillan, who sailed with Peary on the *Roosevelt,* was a leading force in casting off the last vestiges of heroic nineteenth-century exploration over the course of thirty-one trips to Greenland and the Canadian north which ended only in 1957. His best-known expedition, launched from Maine in 1925, undertook to map thirty thousand square miles of the high Arctic from the air, using short-wave radios for communication. MacMillan is credited with paving the way for the over-the-poles flights of Richard Byrd. More than that, however, MacMillan—and his wife Miriam—filmed and photographed native life over a long period of time, providing glimpses of Inuit life at and after the incursion of Euro-American goods and cultural influences.

Rockwell Kent, the American painter and illustrator whose early stay in Maine set the tenor for his future life as a pictorial chronicler of the North, made three separate trips to the west coast of Greenland between 1929 and 1933. Each time, he threw himself into the routines of daily life, building houses, hosting parties, and engaging a native woman as his housekeeper and companion. *Salamina,* published in 1935, describes his mistress in both words and pictures, depicting a kind of Gauguinesque paradise of simplicity, beauty, and grace. In addition to his stories and images of adventures in Alaska, Newfoundland, and Tierra del

Rockwell Kent, *Salamina* coffee pot, 1939

Fuego and his astonishing illustrations for Melville's *Moby-Dick* (1930), Kent also took photographs of the villagers of Greenland working and going about their daily lives in what might otherwise be mistaken for bizarre costumes.

On the one hand, then, Rockwell Kent idealized the Inuit life on the ice because it was unlike the repressions and grasping venality of his own culture—much as the hollow earth school of literature conjured up new/old lands, untouched by the mistakes of "advanced" earthly society. On the other hand, for all his idealization, Kent showed the practical, everyday things the citizens of the North did in clothing that was both functional and—to American eyes—very strange indeed. He straddled two ways of looking at a world so foreign to most Americans as to be the stuff of fiction.

The film that would finally convince the world that the polar region's frozen terrain harbored a culture worthy of the respectful attention of the urbanized Western world was *Nanook of the North,* released in 1922. Although the term was unknown at the time, *Nanook* is said to be the first true documentary. Robert Flaherty, the director, cinematographer, casting agent, and developer of film stock, was by no means a professional movie man. Before he arrived at the village of Inukjuak on the east side of Hudson's Bay in 1920, he had made four long trips to the Canadian Arctic in the employ of Sir William MacKenzie, mine owner and railroad magnate, for whom he drew maps and scouted locations of potential mineral deposits. In the course of these wanderings, Flaherty had frequent contact with the region's Inuit and was captivated not only by their simplicity and grace but by their ability to survive in the most unforgiving physical environment on the planet.

Several years earlier, he had taken a Bell and Howell motion picture camera with him into the frozen wild, but the resulting short film attracted little attention. In June 1920 he came again, equipped for a long stay with professional equipment, seventy-five thousand feet of film stock, a gramophone, his violin, a picture of his wife, and the financial backing of a great fur trading company about to celebrate the two hundredth anniversary of its operations at Hudson's Bay. When Flaherty left a year later, he had the makings of *Nanook of the North.*

Despite the overwhelming success of *Nanook,* which drew worldwide audiences and confounded distributors' initial reservations, critics and documentary "purists" have raised objections to Flaherty's procedures. For one thing, he hand-picked villagers to play parts, to act out a version of their own lives that emphasized family connections and a certain insouciance in the face of hardship. "Nanook" (The Bear), identified in the titles as "Chief of the Itivimuits . . . famous through all Ungava," was a man called Alakariallak, chosen

Movie poster

because he was photogenic, taller than the average Inuit, and familiar with traditional hunting methods, which had been all but replaced by the gun and the motor by 1920. His "wives" were not his wives. One of them, Maggie, renamed "Nyla" or "Smiling One," was picked for her radiant good looks. After Flaherty had gone to New York to edit and promote his film with the help of his American wife, Nyla gave birth to his son, Josephie, with whom he had no contact.

Nanook of the North opens with a staged comic scene. A kayak pulls up to shore. Alakariallak jumps out, smiling broadly. Then, as if by magic, the whole "family" tumbles out of the tiny craft and onto the ice after him: dogs, puppies, children, wives, and a tiny baby girl carried in her mother's fur hood. After the horrors of World War I, such scenes of happy families reinforced the sense that a simple life dominated by human warmth—even in the ice and snowfields—offered a model for the sophisticated moviegoer watching in ease and comfort. Nanook's status as hunter, leader, and protector is also stressed. It is he who instructs his young son on the art of bow hunting. It is he who heaves the cumbersome harpoon. And he who creeps out on the treacherous ice to lure the seal and drag it from the water. This latter scene was carefully staged, too, as a kind of Darwinian struggle between man and nature. The seal was already dead, but lines stretched under the ice allowed for an epic battle in which the hunters are pulled up to the hole and stagger back again, until the beast is finally yanked out of the depths for "slaughter."

The igloo and the heroic Nanook are the movie's central icons. In a remarkable and instructive sequence clearly rehearsed for best effect, Nanook builds an igloo using only a snow knife of walrus ivory to shelter his little band from the elements. Flaherty's own memoirs indicate that it proved impossible to construct an igloo large enough to accommodate the cast and the camera while allowing sufficient light for filming. Thus for interior scenes of the family bedding down for the night, a half-igloo open to the elements was actually used. In 1932, Vilhjalmur Stefansson's secretary reviewed *Nanook of the North* under a headline asking "Is Nanook a Fake?" Of course it was, on one level. Or, as Flaherty put it, "sometimes you have to lie" in order to tell the truth. One truth was that acculturation was already far advanced in Inukjuak when Robert Flaherty began his movie. The ethnographic component of *Nanook* lies chiefly in his ability to persuade Maggie and the others to use the methods and materials of their parents and grandparents.

The **MODERN-DAY ICE ROADS OF THE CANADIAN NORTH** run over a chain of portages, permafrost, and frozen lakes from Yellowknife in the Northwest Territory to remote gold and diamond mines where the temperatures regularly plunge to -70°F. During a short, sixty-day season, eighteen-wheeler semis must deliver a year's worth of supplies and heavy equipment—ten thousand loads—while facing whiteouts, cracks and holes in the ice, engine failure, and the omnipresent danger of plunging through the surface in a fully loaded semi. The surprise hit of the 2007 summer TV season was a weekly series on the triumphs and mishaps of a band of these intrepid drivers making the 350-mile run. *Ice Road Truckers* on the History Channel has all the best features of reality television—suspense, interesting characters, an exotic setting—stripped down to the taut basics, with real lives and livelihoods on the line.

But beyond the "realism" demanded by his critics, Flaherty managed to convey something even more real—the harsh, simple, warm, and often joyous lives of the Inuit of the northern ice. Nanook himself, with his broad smile and almost unconscious feats of athleticism and tenderness, was a real person—not Exhibit A in somebody else's lecture. And the forbidding, barren landscape in which he lives, shot on blue-green sensitive film, is always a pictorial actor in the story, never a papier-mâché iceberg or a mound of artificial snow. Flaherty's is the romantic alternative to cinema verité—suspenseful, moving, and altogether different from any account of the Arctic produced in more than four centuries of intense exploration.

At the South Pole, coincidentally, Frank Hurley was producing his own documentary of the Shackleton expedition, which came to grief when the *Endurance* was crushed by ice in the Weddell Sea in 1914. Hurley's *In the Grip of the Polar Pack Ice* was finally shown in England in 1919, and while it displayed the grit of the British pole-seekers and the fearsome terrain of the "farthest South," the beautiful film lacked the stark contrasts and happy spirit of *Nanook of the North*. One of Flaherty's title cards describes the Inuit of the unyielding Arctic as the "fearless, lovable, happy-go-lucky Eskimo" people. And his film more than proves the contention. History sadly records that Nanook himself died of cold and starvation on a hunt two years after he won the hearts of millions as an unwitting movie star. The ice is cruel. But the smiling Nanook lives on in spirit and in unforgettable images, tinged by the wistful modern hope that somewhere, somehow, beyond the ice, a world of love and happiness might still exist.

As a whole, dramatic Hollywood movies about ice and the culture of ice are a disappointing lot. One of the best is *The Savage Innocents* of 1960, filmed by director Nicholas Ray in Arctic locations and starring Anthony Quinn (an all-purpose ethnic) as an Eskimo hunter living the life of his ancestors, eking out a precarious living by hunting on the tundra. Although "Inuk" is Nanook with dialogue, the character goes beyond the prototype by illustrating the clash between his culture and the habits of a missionary sent to civilize the North. Inuk slays the priest for refusing the favors of his wife, offered according to Eskimo custom. Pursued by the law in the person of Mountie Peter O'Toole (whose lines were overdubbed by a less British voice), *The Savage Innocents* has been hailed as a gritty portrayal—in color—of the punishing geography of the Canadian North and the misunderstandings caused by conflicting mores.

Popular songs equate ice with thrills and strong emotions. Bruce Springsteen's **"ICEMAN"** tells the story of a love-crazed driver steering his Ford toward immortality. Vanilla Ice sings about an "Ice Man party" for the coolest, funkiest fans of 1992. Bob Dylan has stated that "Quinn the Eskimo (The Mighty Quinn)," which he wrote in the late 1960s and performed on the so-called *Basement Tapes*, refers to the Anthony Quinn ice epic, *The Savage Innocents* (1960).

The many later movies whose Arctic settings are basic to their plots fall into several distinct categories: sci-fi with a distinctly scientific edge, heartwarming global warming parables, and Cold War skullduggery. *Iceman* (1984) is a representative example of the scientific genre. Released the year in which a Canadian team made headlines when they uncovered the graves of three members of the Franklin party frozen in the permafrost for 138 years—and concluded that the unfortunate explorers had been poisoned by the lead used to seal their canned foods—*Iceman* concerns a forty-thousand-year-old man found intact in the Arctic ice by scientists in the employ of "Polaris Mining and Chemical." When his ice block thaws, "Charlie" wakes up. One faction wants to learn about human development by building an artificial environment in which he can be studied and befriended. Another wants to dissect him in order to discover the secrets of long-term cryonic preservation. The "good" scientist wears furs and Inuit slit goggles. The "bad" ones favor scrubs and North Face parkas. Again, the frigid setting, the glittering ice, and the small community's isolation bring the definition of humanity into sharp relief. Is modern science better than "primitive" adaptation to the elements? What does the sophisticated present stand to learn from its untutored forebears?

Steven Spielberg's *Artificial Intelligence* (2001) is not an Arctic film per se, but when advanced robotic science fails to produce a duplicate child who can elicit love from his adopted family, the little simulacrum sinks himself into the rapidly freezing waters of New York harbor in despair, a variation on the Frankenstein story. The ice that entombs young Haley Joel Osment speaks to the absence of love and warmth on the part of the flesh-and-blood beings who have rejected their almost-real child. The ice flows from the glacial depths of the human heart.

A.I. takes place against a background of much-debated climate change and global warming, topics that have spilled out of the scientific realm into the media, common discourse, and the classroom. Enter the child-friendly cartoon feature starring a mammoth, a saber-toothed tiger, and a hapless squirrel. *Ice Age* (2002) and its timely sequel, *Ice Age: The Meltdown* (2006), put a quasi-human face on the issues of receding polar ice and rising planetary temperatures by the use of familiar voices from the television screen and the winsome antics of doomed creatures fleeing their icebound habitat. The message could not be clearer: to save the animals, kids need to become guardians of the planet. Recycle! Walk, don't ride in the minivan! Take a closer look at the pictures of the vanishing ice caps in Al Gore's documentary! Pay close attention to the spoken narrative in *The March of the Penguins* as the engaging birds struggle to survive an Antarctic winter! Do your math homework!

By far the most interesting of the ice-and-snow films, however, are those set in the far North after World War II, when the Cold War raged on in the ice of the Northwest Passage and the nuclear superpowers jockeyed for advantage along the shortest bomber routes to each other's heartlands. From the Big Chill of the 1950s and '60s emerged more powerful icebreakers, a new breed of polar satellites, and nuclear submarines capable of stealthy passage from the Atlantic to the Pacific underneath the ice's protective mantle. The North of the Eskimo, the domain of Symmes Holes and open polar seas, became the preserve of the spy. A lavish cinematic tribute to the era of espionage, high-tech weaponry, and ice is the widescreen, full-color classic *Ice Station Zebra,* which premiered in 1968 with an all-male cast of stars headed by Rock Hudson. Russians, Americans, British agents, and double agents tussle in a blizzard as a Soviet trawler loaded with electronic listening devices makes its way toward an isolated research base and the USS *Ronco* (a real U.S. Navy sub borrowed for dramatic under-the-ice shots of bergs dangling down into the sea) closes in from the opposite side. Although meant to be a joint U.S.A./U.S.S.R. rescue operation, it ends in a tense standoff: "Until we meet again," says the Russian commandant as the polar night descends once more upon the ice.

> The **ICE PICK THAT KILLED TROTSKY** came to light in 2005, sixty-five years after it was stolen from the Mexican police. Leon Trotsky, exiled to a suburb of Mexico City in a purge by Stalin, was struck down on August 20, 1940, by Ramon Mercader. The assassin hit Trotsky in the head with the sharpened end of a mountaineering tool. Trotsky's grandson, Seva Volkov, has offered DNA samples for comparison with the bloodstains still visible on the handle.

Ice Station Zebra—"z" stands for the last place on earth—was adapted from a novel by Alistair MacLean, the dean of Cold War potboilers. But a vast range of so-called "beach novels" use various ice-related titles and plots to inspire delicious chills on hot days. All or almost all of the best-selling paperback novelists whose work is featured in airport gum-and-shampoo shops have churned one out: Dan Brown, Michael Crichton, Clive Cussler, Tom Racina, and Matthew Reilly—all the writers, that is, whose disposable "quick-read" books merit frosted, silver-foil covers.

The stories are predictably preposterous. Nazis still alive in dens excavated in the polar ice. Killers loose at the Weddell Station in Antarctica. Floating icebergs with mystery ships embedded in their cores. Fake meteorites planted by NASA deep beneath the frigid surface of Ellesmere Island.

Huge mutant marine mammals guarding undersea ice caverns at the poles. California in the grips of unending subzero weather. And so forth. The words "ice," "freeze," or "iceberg" in the title, a picture of something jagged and white on the cover, and the sale is as good as made. These "new North" novels promise fear, excitement, conspiracy, danger, and a ripping good read. Violence, but not much sex (it's too cold!). Language spiked with equations and the names of mysterious agencies. Maps. Diagrams. Science, assaults on the climate, and bad guys who want to rule the world. Ice is to genre fiction what the white whale was to Ahab, what the albatross was to the Ancient Mariner.

> The **MIRACLE ON ICE** was the 1980 gold medal win by the U.S. hockey team over the seemingly unbeatable Russians at the Winter Olympics in Lake Placid, New York. The team, made up mostly of young collegiate amateurs, was coached by Herb Brooks, a Minnesotan generally credited with being the best hockey coach of all time. Brooks was killed in an automotive rollover in 2003 as he returned to the Twin Cities from a Hockey Hall of Fame fundraiser. "He never saw it. He lived it," read the on-screen dedication at the end of the 2004 movie *Miracle*, starring Kurt Russell as the legendary coach.

Clive Cussler's Dirk Pitt—the hero of *Raise the Titanic!*—is the ideal iceman for the post–Heroic Age of exploration, in which some still believe that Armstrong's moon landing was faked in an aircraft hanger in Utah. Pitt is truly an all-American guy: cool, laconic, ingenious, and tech savvy, a kind of *Playboy* ideal strayed into the twenty-first century. The British approach to polar heroes as portrayed on the silver screen has followed a different course. Their heroes are made of sterner stuff, beginning with *Scott of the Antarctic* (1948), a subdued English production with a soundtrack by the London Philharmonic and a matter-of-fact, stiff-upper-lip performance by John Mills as the ill-fated Robert Falcon Scott. The film's mood is tempered, of course, by the fact that the viewer knows the sad outcome in advance. But there is something more, a British malaise in the aftermath of wartime daring and privations, which never seems to touch the American denizen of the ice. John Wayne's *Island in the Sky* (1953) describes the plight of a former army pilot flying transport missions to secret northern bases. He crash-lands in uncharted territory as an arctic storm bears down on his remote frozen lake. Yet Wayne comes through with barely a shiver, his stardom perhaps insulating him from the tragic outcome of John Mills's adventure in Antarctica.

> UFO buffs and the FAA both collect data on huge chunks of ice—the size of microwave ovens—that fall from the sky without warning and are not the so-called "blue ice" from airplane toilets. Investigators theorize that these **MEGACRYOMETEORS**, at least fifty of which have been recorded since 1999, are a byproduct of global warming: greater temperature differences between warm and cold layers in the upper atmosphere create huge hailstones without the need for thunderstorms.

The Last Place on Earth (1985) and *Shackleton* (2002), both television films aimed at reviving exemplars of the glory days of Scott's long trek to the South Pole, begin from the premise that it may be better to be an Englishman than the first to reach the prize. In the former, the Norwegians and the few odd Americans who figure in the script are a little off somehow: too ambitious, too venal, too obsessed with

Pykrete

During World War II, Lord Louis Mountbatten staged a special demonstration at the Quebec Conference attended by Winston Churchill, Franklin Roosevelt, and their military advisors. Mountbatten displayed two blocks, one of ice and the other made of a mystery substance. When he shot the ice block with his pistol, it shattered dramatically. But the bullet glanced off the second, narrowly missed his air chief, grazed Admiral Ernest King, and buried itself in the wall. This harder-than-hard form of ice was called **PYKRETE** (after the eccentric Geoffrey Pyke of the Royal Navy, its most ardent advocate).

The demonstration convinced the gathering to authorize a program code-named "Project Habakkuk," for building aircraft carriers to guard Allied bases in the Arctic using pykrete, a mixture of 14 percent sawdust or wood pulp and 86 percent water. The slurry, when frozen, was tougher than pure ice and floatable, and it melted slowly, making it ideal, Pyke thought, for immense ships closer in size to islands than to conventional carriers. These so-called bergships, two million tons in weight, up to four thousand feet long and six hundred feet wide, could be built relatively cheaply and quickly. Once afloat, they were practically impervious to bombs and torpedoes. They were, therefore, just the thing for protecting vital Atlantic shipping lanes against German U-boats. Because of the high cost of development, estimated at $100 million for the prototype vessel, Mountbatten and the British hoped to persuade the Americans to take over Project Habakkuk.

A 60-by-30-foot test ship was built in 1943 on an isolated lake in the Canadian Rockies using wooden joists filled with harvested ice. At the same time, further top-secret tests on Lake Louise, in front of the celebrated chateau at Banff, Alberta, determined that a 35-foot hull was necessary to resist extensive damage from explosives. But by the time the experimenting was over, the Battle of the Atlantic had finally swung in favor of the Allies and the notion of a fearsome pykrete fleet was shelved for the duration.

Pykrete survives as a curiosity, a memory, another amazing idea whose time came and went with great rapidity under wartime pressures. To date, no pykrete ships defend our coastline or our active installations in the polar North.

glory. Scott, played by the mild Martin Shaw, and Shackleton, played by the charismatic Kenneth Branagh (former Baron Frankenstein), are just right in their own ways: stoic, uxorious, and loyal in the case of Scott, brave and affable in the case of Shackleton—but very British. In the final analysis, however, neither film brings the lead character to life. In a semi-documentary fashion, Scott is one of a group, sometimes impossible to single out in a crowd. Even Branagh, unlike the standard movie star, does not quite succeed in being the hero of his own story. In movies of World War II that utilized the convention of "families" of fighting men, a Robert Taylor or a John Wayne also represented a father figure. Recent polar docudramas imported from British studios, however, seem more suited to the corporate sensibility and revived nationalism of the Thatcher era. The true British hero survives the ice or dies well fighting its rigors. No fuss. No muss.

The crucible of polar ice has forged a sensibility of extremes, geared to temperatures of -60° F. Exaltation is matched by fear, fact by fiction, primitivism by futuristic science, frostbite and scurvy by dreams of a heaven-on-earth at the bottom of a nonexistent hole in the ocean. Plans go awry. The creaking and hissing of the ice seem almost human—and malevolent. Human beings, if they are to survive, must come to terms with who they are at the essential center of a hollow self protected by rings of ice and the uncharted waters of the open polar seas.

Belmore Browne, *Chief's Canoe*, ca. 1920s

ICY FINGERS UP
AND DOWN MY SPINE

"I'm mel-ting!"

—

Wicked Witch of the West in *The Wizard of Oz* (1939)

As you will have noticed by now, I am no scientist. Perhaps I'll flatter myself here by invoking the name of Robert Falcon Scott, who wasn't much of a scientist either but was, in the end, seduced by the beauty and the awfulness of Antarctic ice. I feel pretty much the same way. Ice scares me—and it makes me feel wildly alive, skin tingling, breath spewing forth in frantic little clouds, glasses frozen to my nose and fogged with rime.

Ice is one of the few things that make the body sense its own edges, strengths, and frailties in a world weaned on spectatorship, air-conditioning, cars, and desk jobs. Ice will never make an athlete out of me, but it does remind me of being a human animal, a creature that shares a lot of common ground with penguins, polar bears, and Scott of the Antarctic. Despite Scott's disappointing death, ice reminds me of the mutable joys of being alive. A part of which is death.

The literature and subliterature I love tends to pile up on the outer edges of things—where monsters go to perish, where whales still rule the depths, where poor souls make their last flight for freedom across frozen waters. Even the clumsiest Nazis-at-the-Pole novels define the absolute limits of humankind. Beyond the *Pequod,* nature rules and the affairs of mortals produce only ruin. There is a certain doleful poetry in the artless prose of those who remind us that global warming is probably our own fault.

In 2007, former vice president Al Gore won the Nobel Peace Prize for his campaign to address the issue of global warming. Daily newspapers and TV schedules were suddenly clogged with alarming stories about polar ice or the lack thereof. In the summer of the previous year, a Russian naval officer dropped a replica of his nation's flag to the bottom of an ice-free Northwest Passage, thus claiming the newly open sea route to India—and the oil reserves hidden beneath—for his nation. If that were not enough to rattle Washington, Ottawa, and London, the word from the scientists was even more troublesome. "A Vicious Climate Circle" read a headline out of Toronto: the polar ice melt in the North exposes more seawater to sunlight, raising global temperatures and desiccating woodlands, thus spreading drought, which causes wildfires and atmospheric pollution. And so on. And so on. The United Nations hastily convened a climate summit in hopes of shaming the United States into supporting mandatory carbon-based fuel emission cuts to break the cycle of melting. That ploy failed.

The shrinking Arctic ice cap, said the *New York Times,* "Unnerves the Experts." Polar scientists from NASA to Norway and Siberia wondered if the process had "passed a point where it's becoming essentially irreversible." Gretel Ehrlich, who is not given to statistical tables in support of her poetic appreciation of the far North, nonetheless notes that since 1850—or the beginning of the Industrial Revolution—the area of the planet covered by glaciers has diminished by 75 percent. British explorer Pen Hadow, after testing his underwater surveying equipment in a pond in London's Hyde Park, set off to take ten million readings of ice thickness between Point Barrow, Alaska, and the North Pole early in 2008.

The same kind of work is going forward at the South Pole, with similar results. It is no longer prudent to dismiss portents of disaster as the daydreams of crazy, tree-hugging liberals out to ruin the market for Detroit SUVs. Yet that neocon view of the potentially catastrophic ice melt is prevalent enough to make a sane person wonder if ideology leads

Ice out, 1915

inevitably to idiocy. When *Happy Feet,* a cartoon for kids, hit the multiplex in 2006, a Fox TV host called the story of a tap-dancing penguin an "animated *Inconvenient Truth"* because the cute-as-buttons Antarctic bird population aimed to clean up the human-generated garbage polluting their pristine ice shelf. The same commentator said that he "half-expected to see an animated version of Al Gore pop up." Conservative movie maven Michael Medved—who seems to have forgotten all about the shooting of Bambi's mother—called *Happy Feet* the "darkest, most disturbing feature length animated film ever offered by a major studio." A new Frankenstein monster is stalking the ice these days, and it is not an animated version of Al Gore.

Minnesota's Polar Explorers

Minnesota is a modern-day hotbed of **POLAR EXPLORA-TION.** Will Steger from Ely, Minnesota, led a celebrated trek to the North Pole in 1986. Like the Heroic Age adventurers before them, the Steger expedition went with dogs and sleds (and deliberately did without airlifts or resupply). In part, this chosen austerity was a way of testing whether Robert Peary could have reached the pole in 1909 similarly equipped. A team of six eventually completed the thousand-mile journey in fifty-five days, reaffirming the daring and self-sufficiency of the polar pioneers. More important, perhaps, was the composition of Steger's thoroughly international group. Included also was Ann Bancroft, another Minnesotan, who became the first woman ever to reach the North Pole. Steger and his colleague Paul Schurke dedicated their account of the journey to Mat-

thew Henson, the African American who was the unsung
hero of the Peary expedition.

In 1990, Steger completed a transcontinental push
across Antarctica by foot, with a company of scientists,
sled dog handlers, and men from six different nations in
another plea for global cooperation. Both Steger and Bancroft, in subsequent forays onto the polar ice at both ends
of the world, have taken pains to keep in touch with school-
children—to educate those who follow their adventures
about the dire consequences of warming temperatures
and ice melt. Indeed, they have served as eyewitnesses to
climate change as it occurs. And they have sometimes
been its victims. Bancroft, for example, was forced to abort
her trek in 2007 because of frostbite and unexpectedly *cold*
spring temperatures. In 2006, Lonnie Dupre and Eric Lar-
sen, also from Minnesota, were evacuated from the Arctic
Ocean by helicopter when the ice suddenly melted. The
following year found Steger above the Arctic Circle once
again, with Sir Richard Branson and a group of Inuit, publicly bemoaning the scarcity of glaciers, the general insta-
bility of the sea ice, and the breakup which has come earlier
and earlier over the past several decades.

The repeated mention of ice in the media, however, has
been enough to set off a kind of nostalgia-driven embrace of
ice by Americans and Europeans wealthy enough to indulge
in retro-tourism. Antarctic boat tours via decommissioned
Russian icebreakers are pricey and popular. Newfoundland, where times have been tough since the cod fisheries
collapsed in the 1980s, has found a new growth industry in
iceberg tours and all their attendant paraphernalia: pretty,

soft-focus photos of bergs backlit against the dawn, berg sweatshirts, and vials of ice meltwater. Imagine the local uproar in the summer of 1998, then, when a barge equipped with a large crane slipped into a harbor on the north coast, tethered itself to an iceberg, and methodically chipped away at the beautiful blue cathedral of the seas with a grapple. The extractive business, led by Iceberg Industries (est. 1996), had come to Newfoundland.

The barge soon sailed away with twelve hundred tons of glacial ice bound for the company's tank farm further south. There the meltwater is stored for bottling, distilling, and finishing premium vodka. Soon, an executive confided to a reporter, the firm hoped to send out scout planes in search of promising icebergs and to build a floating bottling plant where the whole process could be carried out at sea. Earlier forays into the meltwater trade by the Canadian Iceberg Vodka Company, he added, had been hampered by backward technology. In the old days, fishing boats would land men on a berg with chain saws lubricated with bottles of vegetable oil. They would lop off chunks, secure them in nets, and haul them aboard. The work was dangerous—it is in the nature of icebergs to flip over with no warning— and costly. The yield of ice was small. Now, with modern equipment, the harvest season could last from April until the end of November and the cutting crew was reduced to two workers who never set foot on the ice.

As awareness of the climate crisis spreads, there has been no shortage of suggestions about how to reverse global warming (and thus forestall hurricane formation). One of the most outlandish involves towing icebergs to the tropics to lower sea temperatures there. The related notion of moving huge quantities of ice to provide drinking water for arid regions surfaced in a big way in 1977, at an eighteen-nation International Conference on Iceberg Utilization convened at Iowa State University. The sponsor of the gathering was then Prince Mohammed al Faisal of Saudi Arabia, CEO of Iceberg Transport International. He wanted to find a 100-million-pound iceberg off Antarctica, wrap it up in plastic, and tow it to the Arabian Peninsula for use as drinking water (an estimated eight months' worth). Meltwater from icebergs is potable, of course, because it is made from successive layers of pristine snow, densely compacted by its own weight. Hence Australia, Kuwait, Namibia, and California have all entertained the notion of towing icebergs to supply their needs. As late as 2006, the Thames Water Authority floated a plan to tow icebergs down from northern Scandinavia to ease shortages.

> For an exhibition in Jerusalem in 1999, flamboyant glass sculptor Dale Chihuly proposed a conventional show of shaped glass pieces in the Tower of David Museum and an ice installation outside the citadel's walls. The ICE WALL WAS DESIGNED TO MELT AWAY within a week, changing color as it disappeared and symbolizing "melting tensions" in the Middle East. One of the component parts was a giant sixty-four-ton ice sphere mined in Fairbanks, Alaska, and shipped to Israel cushioned in sawdust. Earlier Chihuly works used neon tubes embedded in ice and an ice chandelier perched atop a huge boulder at Sleeping Lady Mountain Retreat in Washington State.

The hitch, of course, is that the energy needed to run the giant towboats—one hopeful entrepreneur suggested borrowing the carrier *Iwo Jima* from the U.S. Navy—would make water more expensive glass for glass than vintage champagne. And the pollution created by the smoke billowing from the ships' stacks would more than outweigh any benefits accrued from taking advantage of existing freshwater supplies instead of building desalinization plants. Leave it to an athletic Brit to volunteer to move bergs by eco-friendly wind power, using giant kites to sail the ice home while battling seasickness, the slippage of anchor points, emerging crevasses, and the omnipresent danger of turnover. He allowed as how his survival depended on "staying very alert" at all times; one of the most dangerous jobs on earth belongs to the specialists who lasso icebergs and tow them away from oil rigs in bad weather to prevent further ecological disasters.

One major flaw in the towboat scenario has been pointed out many times—namely, that the boat (or kite) will arrive in port dangling an empty line behind it. The iceberg will have melted away, sharing the fate of the thousands calved each year from the Ross or the Wedell Sea or the Greenland ice shelves. Such is the nature of one of the most beautiful things on earth: it will disappear. In the autumn of 2007, the U.S. Postal Service issued a twenty-stamp block of first-class commemoratives called "Polar Lights." There are two designs in the set, one showing the aurora borealis of the North Pole and the other the aurora australis of the South. Vaguely reminiscent of Frederic Church ice paintings, they are as spectacular as a 1¼-inch width will permit. But they are ominously different.

The borealis stamps show a distinct *land*scape: mountains, trees, reflective coastal waters—surmounted by a swirl of pastel lights. The australis stamps, by contrast, feature a cluster of deep blue icebergs afloat on a sapphire sea, against a backdrop of brilliant reds and greens, arranged in vertical bands. The scene could have come straight from "Con" Scott's journal, suffused with majesty and awe. The Postal Service, then, seems to have pretty much given up on the North Pole. In the philatelic world, the North is a kind of chillier Colorado improved by a show of neon lights while the South Pole is still a place of wonderment and mystery. Its lights shoot up straight out of the primordial ice as if to touch the rim of heaven. What ice remains to us is magical, beautiful beyond our power to tell, a memory buried deep inside the core of our being, like a core of ancient ice dredged up by some divine polar poet.

Ice formation, Duluth, 1910

Ice has more mundane dimensions, too. Ice is a memory of apple-red cheeks—of gigantic ice ladies carved on the front lawn, hockey skates, pistachio ice-cream cones scooped out from the depths of a wheezing freezer, icicles dangling from gutters, ice cubes tinkling in a cocktail shaker (never, never stir!). Coming in from the cold as ice crystals sparkle in the air. Sentiments frozen in time like so many chilled Sara Lee madeleines of the soul. Ice is a metaphor for finding the self in the contemplation of profound otherness; warm-blooded creatures need the ice on Walden Pond to understand what they are or what they could be.

Minnesotans need fish houses on frozen lakes and record low temperatures and ice storms to remind themselves of just how special they are. Ice is to the denizens of the northern plains what snow is to upstate New York—a mark of honor, unearned but deeply appreciated. Ice and cities don't mingle nicely. Ice is the earth's secret agent, stealing indoors through the dispenser in the hole-in-the-door, side-by-side refrigerator. Civilization may well end in ice of its own making. Or not.

> Although it may seem a little strange to Arizonans, **ICE FISHING** is a major form of outdoor recreation in states along our northern borders. It can be as simple as a fellow in earmuffs sitting on an overturned bucket or as elaborate as a deluxe portable fish house with nine holes for lines, bunk beds, satellite TV, pine paneling, an electronic "fish alert," and a full-size gas range, all for $6,881 plus extras. The annual Eelpout Festival on Leech Lake in Walker, Minnesota, holds a contest for the best customized house. Participants construct mostly male neighborhoods with streets, golf courses, and other ice-bound amenities.

If you live up here in the Frozen North, your favorite movie is or is not *Fargo* (1996), a comedic murder story filmed by ex-Minnesotans Joel and Ethan Coen in the town of Brainerd, one of those rare wintertime resorts without a ski lift. This resort status dates from the 1930s, when the Depression kept motorists away from the usual Minnesota summer pleasures of swimming, boating, and fishing. In the winter of '37, the situation bottomed out. A persistent north wind drove the temperatures to -30 degrees and kept them there. In despair, the town fathers of Bemidji built themselves a giant, awkward likeness of Paul Bunyan, the mythical logger, on the shores of frozen Lake Bemidji. He had a hinged arm to wave at passersby and soon acquired a sidekick: Babe the Blue Ox, who, mounted on the chassis of an old Model A, could scoot down to the Twin Cities to entice visitors to

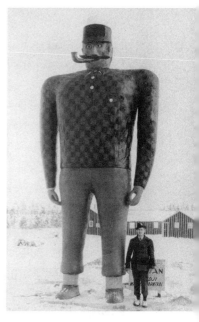

Paul Bunyan at Bemidji, 1938

a new, improved Bemidji and its new Winter Sports Festival. The statuary—fixed and mobile—even rated a picture in *Life* magazine.

Well, that was all too much for Brainerd, about eighty miles south of Bemidji and pretty darn cold itself during ice fishing season. After a suitable interval of grousing and plotting, civic leaders there decided to buy a secondhand, thirty-six-foot-tall, five-thousand-pound *talking* figure, which, when dressed in a size seventy-three wool plaid shirt and size eighty boots, played the part of Paul Bunyan on the shores of the local lake. And for more than half a century, this Paul scared Minnesota kids silly when he bobbed his enormous head, peered down, and greeted each one by name in a booming amplified voice. He's a kind of folkloric Frankenstein monster in plaid, doomed to haunt the icy expanses of Minnesota's ten thousand lakes in search of lucrative motel reservations for the spring "ice-out" season.

Fargo, with its frozen-faced Paul Bunyan, is not really Fargo, North Dakota, but Brainerd—a desolate, glacial ice sheet on the prairie enlivened by occasional glimpses of the ghastly, ghostly figure of Paul Bunyan, by hideous murders, and by the unfailing pluck and determination of the pregnant local sheriff. If the statue is death by ice, then the cheery Chief Gunderson is life, warm and tart as a new-picked apple. If Paul Bunyan is frozen folklore, the folksy Marge Gunderson is the genuine article. The credits for the movie claim that the plot is based on real events. That isn't true. Neither Bemidji nor Brainerd, despite their rivalries, is the kind of town where corpses litter the ice (unless they have been carefully ground to bits in a wood-chipper). They are towns where folks know who they are, what's right, and what's not. As hard and cold as the ice of winter may be, they wouldn't have it any other way.

Frankenstein isn't real. *Fargo* isn't quite real, either. But Brainerd is. So is ice.

THANK YOU!

No author is an island—or an iceberg floating alone on a cold and lonely sea. I had lots of help in calving this book. Greg Britton at Borealis Books had the idea in the first place; a rip-roaring Minnesota winter will often bring thoughts of Arctic climes to mind. Stuart Klipper's breathtaking Antarctic photography was a constant inspiration—especially a picture he sent to me years ago showing Elvis (a cardboard Elvis!) adrift on an ice floe. Jean Spraker generously lent me her files, the result of years of meticulous research on the culture of winter carnivals here and in Canada. Helen A. Harrison shared her marvelous essay on the history of ice boating. Liz Dotson called my attention to Craig Blacklock's stunning images of the ice on Lake Superior. Julie Bernson at the Phillips Academy's Addison Gallery of American Art showed me the museum's important collection of polar art. Paul Knoke sent along an ancestral memoir on ice harvesting. Lauren Soth, after a day of art-looking in Washington, DC, kindly reminded me of Joseph Cornell's mysterious jewel box full of artificial ice. My brother, Gregory Marling, contributed his expertise in the field of ice roads for loggers. Erika Doss convinced me that the secret of ice manufacture was to be found in tropical Florida. Richard Fred Arey and Jim Roe provided timely advice, along with Jeffrey Ogbar and Kalyani Fernando. Colleen Sheehy took me to visit Maine's eye-opening Peary-Macmillan Arctic Museum at Bowdoin College. Finally, Kurt Schulz urged me to look into grants-in-aid for spending time in Antarctica. Of course, I paid the price for not going—namely, a very hot, sticky summer in Minneapolis. Nothing is hotter and stickier than that.

A VERY SHORT
ICE GLOSSARY

Like corporate executives, mountain climbers, and cops, people who cope with natural ice on a regular basis have developed a descriptive vocabulary of terms in order to communicate with one another as precisely as possible. Lots of the words are Russian ones. Some words are used on lakes and land as well as the open sea. Some are almost self-explanatory. As is often the case with specialized vocabularies, however, the in-group is fond of tossing unfamiliar phraseology into conversations with non-initiates, which makes for tough sledding if you are an armchair adventurer, trying to slog across Antarctica "sastrugi" or pursue a Nazi submarine beneath the "bummocks" of the polar ice cap. A list of all these mystifying words would run to many volumes. But a select few especially nifty ones may be useful for slipping into casual conversation when the host asks if you want that scotch on the rocks.

Sastrugi. Ridges formed on snow-covered ice by wind erosion. These tend to run parallel to the direction of the prevailing wind that formed them. A grave annoyance to those attempting to haul sleds.

Shuga. Spongy white ice lumps or a kind of new ice formed when slush at sea rises to the surface in the process of freezing.

Pancake ice. Circular floating shapes with raised rims created by pieces banging into one another. May form on a swell of shuga during the action of waves or swells.

Ice cake. A flat piece of sea ice less than twenty meters across.

Bergy bit. A largish hunk of floating ice "calved" from a glacier.

Growler. A little chunk of floating ice, smaller than a bergy bit. These are transparent but often look green or black as they bob along.

Ice shelf. A very large floating ice sheet sometimes as tall as a mountain, still attached to the coastline.

Tabular berg. Any flat-topped iceberg. Most are calved from an ice shelf and display horizontal bands of color.

Nip. The action of ice forcibly pressing in on a ship, sometimes crushing it.

Beset. What happens to a ship surrounded on all sides by ice and unable to move. Icebound.

Bummock. A projection dangling down from the surface of floating ice and a hazard to submarines. If the projection points up from the surface, disrupting the movement of ships and sledding parties, it is called a hummock.

Floeberg. A huge piece of sea ice made up of hummocks frozen together.

Ice field. A substantial area of floating ice.

Ice floe. Floating ice smaller than an ice field.

Polyna. An opening enclosed on all sides by floating ice.

Lead. Navigable passage through the ice cover created by currents or wind.

Ice core. A tall, vertical section bored through an ice sheet. The resulting core contains the ice's incremental history in the form of isotopes, deposits, and bands of color.

SELECTED BIBLIOGRAPHY

1. ICE SWEET ICE

Arnold, Shannon Jackson. *Everybody Loves Ice Cream: The Whole Scoop on America's Favorite Treat.* Cincinnati, OH: Emmis Books, 2004.

Ecott, Tim. *Vanilla.* New York: Grove Press, 2004.

Funderburg, Anne Cooper. *Chocolate, Strawberry, and Vanilla: A History of American Ice Cream.* Bowling Green, OH: Bowling Green University Popular Press, 1995.

Gosnell, Mariana. *Ice: The Nature, the History, and the Uses of an Astonishing Substance.* New York: Knopf, 2005.

Heimann, Jim. *California Crazy and Beyond: Roadside Vernacular Architecture.* San Francisco, CA: Chronicle Books, 2001.

Marling, Karal Ann. *The Colossus of Roads: Myth and Symbol along the American Highway.* Minneapolis: University of Minnesota Press, 1984.

Tice, Patricia M. *Ice Cream for All.* Rochester, NY: The Strong Museum, 1990.

Vaccaro, Pamela J. *Beyond the Ice Cream Cone: The Whole Scoop on Food at the 1904 World's Fair.* St. Louis, MO: Enid Press, 2004.

2. OVER THE ICE

Alighieri, Dante. *The Divine Comedy I: Inferno.* Translated by Robin Kirkpatrick. New York: Penguin, 2006.

——. *The Inferno.* Translated by John Ciardi. New York: Signet, 1982.

Csida, Joseph, and June Bundy. *American Entertainment: A Unique History of Popular Show Business.* New York: Watson-Guptill, 1978.

Everson, William K. *American Silent Film.* New York: Oxford University Press, 1978.

Gates, Henry Louis, Jr., ed. *The Annotated* Uncle Tom's Cabin. New York: W. W. Norton, 2007.

Lott, Eric. *Love and Theft: Blackface Minstrelsy and the American Working Class.* New York: Oxford University Press, 1995.

Maxtone-Graham, John. *Safe Return Doubtful: The Heroic Age of Polar Exploration.* New York: Barnes & Noble, 1999.

Pierce, David. "Commentary." Appended to DVD of *Uncle Tom's Cabin.* 1927. KINO Video, 1999.

Stowe, Harriet Beecher. *Uncle Tom's Cabin, or Life Among the Lowly.* Edited by Ann Douglas. New York: Penguin, 1986.

3. ROMANTIC ICE

Addison Gallery of American Art: 65 Years. New York: D.A.P., 1996.

Bach, Steven. *Leni: The Life and Work of Leni Riefenstahl.* New York: Knopf, 2007.

Carr, Gerald L. *Frederic Edwin Church: The Icebergs.* Dallas, TX: Dallas Museum of Fine Arts, 1980.

Harvey, Eleanor Jones. *The Voyage of the Icebergs: Frederic Church's Arctic Masterpiece.* New Haven, CT: Yale University Press, 2002.

Huntington, David C. *The Landscapes of Frederic Edwin Church.* New York: Braziller, 1966.

Kavenna, Joanna. *The Ice Museum: In Search of the Lost Land of Thule.* New York: Viking, 2006.

Scott, Robert Falcon. *Journals.* Edited by Max Jones. New York: Oxford, 2005.

Shelley, Mary. *Frankenstein.* Edited by J. Paul Hunter. New York: W. W. Norton, 1996.

———. *Frankenstein.* Edited by Wendy Steiner. New York: Modern Library, 1999.

Stufford, Francis. *I May Be Some Time: Ice and the English Imagination.* New York: Picador, 1997.

Wilson, Andrew, and Tim Barringer. *American Sublime: Landscape Painting in the United States, 1820–1880.* Princeton, NJ: Princeton University Press, 2002.

Wilson, Eric G. *The Spiritual History of Ice: Romanticism, Science, and the Imagination.* New York: Palgrove MacMillan, 2003.

4. ICE MADE, ICE FOUND, ICE SOLD

Buxbaum, Tim. *Icehouses.* Buckinghamshire, UK: Shire Publications, 2002.

Compilation of Works of Art . . . in the United States Capitol. Washington, DC: GPO, 1965.

Cooper, Gail. *Air-Conditioning America: Engineers and the Controlled Environment, 1900–1960.* Baltimore, MD: Johns Hopkins University Press, 1998.

Hicks, Louise Van Nostrand. "Our Life on the Farm, 1892–1910." Unpublished manuscript, ca. 1970, in the collection of Paul Knoke, Rochester, NY.

Hill, Dewey D., and Elliott R. Hughes. *Ice Harvesting in Early America.* New Hartford, NY: New Hartford Historical Society, 1977.

Sherlock, V. M. *The Fever Man: A Biography of Dr. John Gorrie.* Tallahassee, FL: Medallion Press, 1982.

Steinbeck, John. *East of Eden.* New York: Penguin Books, 2002.

Thoreau, Henry David. *Walden.* Edited by Jeffrey S. Cramer. New Haven, CT: Yale University Press, 2006.

Weightman, Gavin. *The Frozen-Water Trade: A True Story.* New York: Hyperion, 2003.

White, John H. *The Great Yellow Fleet: A History of American Railroad Refrigerator Cars.* San Marino, CA: Golden West Books, 1986.

Zabriskie, George A. *John Gorrie, M.D.: Inventor of Artificial Refrigeration.* Ormond Beach, FL: privately printed, 1950.

5. ICE CASTLES

Anderes, Fred, and Ann Agranoff. *Ice Palaces.* New York: Abbeville Press, 1983.

Anisimov, Evgenii V. *Five Empresses: Court Life in Eighteenth-Century Russia.* Westport, CT: Praeger, 2004.

Berton, Pierre. *The Arctic Grail: The Quest for the North West Passage and the North Pole, 1818–1909.* New York: The Lyons Press, 2001.

Curtiss, Mina. *A Forgotten Empress: Anna Ivanovna and Her Era.* New York: Fredrick Ungar, 1974.

Fagan, Brian. *The Little Ice Age: How Climate Made History.* New York: Basic Books, 2000.

Fitzgerald, F. Scott. *The Stories of F. Scott Fitzgerald.* Edited by Malcolm Cowley. New York: Charles Scribner's Sons, 1951.

Harris, Moira F. *Fire & Ice: The History of the Saint Paul Winter Carnival.* St. Paul, MN: Pogo Press, 2003.

Larson, Paul Clifford. *Icy Pleasures: Minnesota Celebrates Winter.* Afton, MN: Afton Historical Society Press, 1998.

Millett, Larry. *Sherlock Holmes and the Ice Palace Murders.* New York: Penguin, 1998.

6. ICEBERGS

Biel, Steven. *Down with the Old Canoe: A Cultural History of the* Titanic *Disaster.* New York: W. W. Norton, 1996.

Biel, Steven, ed. *Titanica: The Disaster of the Century in Poetry, Song, and Prose.* New York: W. W. Norton, 1998.

Crane, David. *Scott of the Antarctic: A Life of Courage and Tragedy.* New York: Alfred A. Knopf, 2006.

Dolin, Eric Jay. *Leviathan: The History of Whaling in America.* New York: W. W. Norton, 2007.

Ehrlich, Gretel. *The Future of Ice: A Journey into Cold.* New York: Vintage, 2004.

Gore, Al. *An Inconvenient Truth.* Emmaus, PA: Rodale, 2006.

Hoeg, Peter. *Smilla's Sense of Snow.* New York: Delta, 1995.

Lopez, Barry. *Arctic Dreams.* New York: Vintage, 2001.

Lord, Walter. *A Night to Remember.* New York: Henry Holt, 1955.

Lynch, Don. *Titanic: An Illustrated History.* New York: Hyperion, 1998.

Melville, Herman. *Moby-Dick, or The Whale.* Illustrated by Rockwell Kent. New York: Modern Library, 2000.

———. *Tales, Poems, and Other Writings.* Edited by John Bryant. New York: Modern Library, 2002.

Monteath, Colin. *Antarctica: Beyond the Southern Ocean.* Aukland, NZ: David Bateman Ltd., 1996.

Myers, Joan. *Wondrous Cold: An Antarctic Journey.* Washington, DC: Smithsonian Books, 2006.

Niven, Jennifer. *The Ice Master.* New York: Hyperion, 2000.

Parry, Richard. *Trial by Ice: The True Story of Murder and Survival on the 1871 Polaris Expedition.* New York: Ballentine Books, 2001.

Stone, Gregory S. *Ice Island: Expedition to Antarctica's Largest Iceberg.* Washington, DC: National Geographic Society, ca. 2001.

Verne, Jules. *20,000 Leagues Under the Sea.* New York: Sterling Publishing, 2006.

7. EXHIBITING ICE AND ICE PEOPLE

Appleton, Victor (pseudo. of E. Stratemeyer). *Tom Swift in the Caves of Ice.* New York: Grosset and Dunlap, ca. 1911.

David, Robert G. *The Arctic in the British Imagination, 1818–1914.* New York: Manchester University Press, 2000.

The Greatest of Expositions: 1904 Saint Louis World's Fair Completely Illustrated. St. Louis, MO: Louisiana Purchase Exposition, 1904.

Harper, Kenn. *Give Me My Father's Body: The Life of Minik, the New York Eskimo.* South Royalton, VT: Steerforth Press, 2000.

Harris, Neil, et al. *Grand Illusions: Chicago World's Fair of 1893.* Chicago, IL: Chicago Historical Society, 1993.

Karp, Ivan, and Steven D. Lavine, eds. *Exhibiting Cultures: The Poetics and Politics of Museum Display.* Washington, DC: Smithsonian Institution, 1991.

Niven, Jennifer. *Ada Blackjack: A True Story of Survival in the Arctic.* New York: Hyperion, 2003.

Robinson, Michael F. *The Coldest Crucible: Arctic Exploration and American Culture*. Chicago, IL: University of Chicago Press, 2006.

Rydell, Robert W. *All the World's a Fair: Visions of Empire at American International Expositions, 1876–1916*. Chicago, IL: University of Chicago Press, 1984.

Rydell, Robert W., and Nancy Gwinn, eds. *Fair Representations: World's Fairs and the Modern World*. Amsterdam: VU University Press, 1994.

Yankielun, Norbert E. *How to Build an Igloo and Other Snow Shelters*. New York: W. W. Norton, 2007.

8. HOLES IN THE ICE

Alexander, Caroline. *The Endurance: Shackleton's Legendary Antarctic Expedition*. New York: Alfred A. Knopf, 1999.

Ehrlich, Gretel. *This Cold Heaven: Seven Seasons in Greenland*. New York: Vintage Books, 2003.

Ferris, Scott, and Ellen Pearce. *Rockwell Kent's Forgotten Landscape: An Artist's Gifts to the Former Soviet Union*. Camden, ME: Down East Books, 1998.

Godwin, Jocelyn. *Arktos: The Polar Myth*. London: Thames & Hudson, 1993.

Griffiths, Tom. *Slicing the Silence: Voyaging to Antarctica*. Cambridge, MA: Harvard University Press, 2007.

Kent, Rockwell. *Salamina*. 1935. Reprint, Middletown, CT: Wesleyan University Press, 2003.

Kent, Rockwell, illus. *Moby-Dick, or The Whale*, by Herman Melville. 1930. Reprint, New York: Random House, 1992.

Martin, Constance. *Distant Shores: The Odyssey of Rockwell Kent*. Los Angeles, CA: Chameleon Books, 2000.

McGrath, Melanie. *The Long Exile: A Tale of Inuit Betrayal and Survival in the High Arctic*. New York: Knopf, 2007.

Serving Art: Rockwell Kent's Salamina Dinnerware. Minneapolis, MN: Frederick R. Weisman Art Museum, 1996.

Stafford, Edward P. *Peary and His Promised Land.* Eagle Island, ME: Friends of Peary's Eagle Island, 1998.

Standish, David. *Hollow Earth.* Cambridge, MA: Da Capo Press, 2006.

Tyler-Lewis, Kelly. *The Lost Men: The Harrowing Saga of Shackleton's Ross Sea Party.* New York: Viking, 2006.

ADDITIONAL SOURCES

Andra-Warner, Elle. *Robert Service: A Great Poet's Romance with the North.* Canmore, Alberta: Altitude Publishing, 2004.

Arnesen, Liv, and Ann Bancroft with Cheryl Dahle. *No Horizon So Far: Two Women and the Extraordinary Journey Across Antarctica.* Cambridge, MA: Da Capo Press, 2003.

Bickel, Lennard. *Mawson's Will: The Greatest Polar Survival Story Ever Written.* Hanover, NH: Steerforth Press, 2000.

Blacklock, Craig and Honey. *A Voice Within: The Lake Superior Nudes.* Moose Lake, MN: Blacklock Photography Galleries, 2004.

Bowen, Mark. *Thin Ice: Unlocking the Secrets of Climate in the World's Highest Mountains.* New York: Henry Holt, 2005.

Cavell, Edward, and Dennis Reid. *When Winter Was King: The Image of Winter in 19th Century Canada.* Banff, Alberta: Altitude Publishing, 1988.

Cherry-Garrard, Aspley. *The Worst Journey in the World: Antarctic 1910–1913.* Washington, DC: National Geographic Society, 2002.

Dregni, Eric. *Zamboni: The Coolest Machines on Ice.* St. Paul, MN: MBI Publishing, 2006.

Krakauer, Jon. *Into Thin Air: A Personal Account of the Mt. Everest Disaster.* New York: Anchor, 1997.

Libbrecht, Kenneth. *The Snowflake: Winter's Secret Beauty.* Stillwater, MN: Voyageur Press, 2003.

Macdougall, Doug. *Frozen Earth: The Once and Future Story of Ice Ages.* Berkeley: University of California Press, 2004.

Pielou, E. C. *After the Ice Age: The Return of Life to Glaciated North America.* Chicago, IL: University of Chicago Press, 1991.

Poor, Henry Varnum. *An Artist Sees Alaska*. New York: Viking, 1945.

Pretor-Pinney, Gavin. *The Cloudspotter's Guide*. New York: Penguin, 2006.

Reinhard, John. *Discovering the Inca Ice Maiden*. Washington, DC: National Geographic Society, 1998.

Simmons, Dan. *The Terror*. New York: Little, Brown and Co., 2007.

Sobey, Ed. *A Field Guide to Household Technology*. Chicago, IL: Chicago Review Press, 2007.

Steger, Will, and Jon Bowermaster. *Crossing Antarctica*. New York: Alfred A. Knopf, 1992.

Steger, Will, with Paul Schurke. *North to the Pole*. New York: Times Books, 1987.

Winchester, Simon. *Outposts: Journeys to the Surviving Relics of the British Empire*. New York: Perennial, 2003.

Young, James A., and Jerry Budy. *Endless Tracks in the Woods*. Sarasota, FL: Crestline Publishing, n.d.

INDEX

ILLUSTRATION CREDITS

PAGE 18 Missouri Historical Society, St. Louis, Montague Lyon Collection

PAGE 21 Eskimo Pie Collection, Archives Center, National Museum of American History, Smithsonian Institution

PAGE 22 reproduced by permission of The Huntington Library, San Marino, California

PAGE 23 Wichita-Sedgwick County Historical Museum

PAGES 29, 109, 129, 165, 169 Library of Congress

PAGE 30 courtesy Special Collections, University of Virginia Library

PAGE 35 courtesy of American Musical Theatre of San Jose, DavidAllenStudio.com

PAGE 48 Oil on canvas, Dallas Museum of Art, anonymous gift

PAGES 52, 121 Addison Gallery of American Art, Phillips Academy, Andover, Massachusetts

PAGE 55 The Metropolitan Museum of Art, Gift of John Stewart Kennedy, 1897 (97.34), image © The Metropolitan Museum of Art

PAGE 56 ImageState stock photo

PAGE 60 © Tate, London, 2007

PAGE 70 National Statuary Hall Collection, Architect of the Capitol

PAGE 78 Maine Historical Society

PAGE 96 © McCord Museum M998X.5.1.6

PAGE 101 Art & Architecture Collection, Miriam and Ira D. Wallach Division of Art, Prints and Photographs, The New York Public Library, Astor, Lenox and Tilden Foundations

PAGE 118 Oxford/RFS Journals

PAGE 122 courtesy Stuart Klipper

PAGE 136 Titanic Historical Society, Inc., and Titanic Museum

PAGE 140 Keystone / AP Photo / Jason Roberts, Push Pictures

PAGE 144 The Library Company of Philadelphia

PAGE 147 Fine Arts Museum of San Francisco, Museum purchase, Achenbach Foundation for Graphic Arts Tribute Fund, 1993.2

PAGE 149 Denver Public Library, Western History Collection, Signal Corp, TMd-394

PAGE 152 Special Collections Research Center, University of Chicago Library

PAGE 158 St. Louis Public Library

PAGE 167 Rockwell Kent, *Salamina* (coffee pot), 1939, vitreous china. Collection of the Frederick R. Weisman Art Museum, University of Minnesota, Minneapolis. Gift of Professor and Mrs. Werner Smith

PAGE 181 Smithsonian American Art Museum, Washington, DC / Art Resource, NY

All other images from Minnesota Historical Society collections